NEW DIR

Arthur M
EDITOR

Florence B. Brawer
ASSOCIATE EDITOR

Assessment and Testing: Myths and Realities

Trudy H. Bers
Oakton Community College

Mary L. Mittler
Oakton Community College

EDITORS

Number 88, Winter 1994

JOSSEY-BASS PUBLISHERS
San Francisco

Clearinghouse for Community Colleges

ASSESSMENT AND TESTING: MYTHS AND REALITIES
Trudy H. Bers, Mary L. Mittler (eds.)
New Directions for Community Colleges, no. 88
Volume XXII, number 4
Arthur M. Cohen, Editor-in-Chief
Florence B. Brawer, Associate Editor

Microfilm copies of issues and articles are available in 16mm and 35mm, as well as microfiche in 105mm, through University Microfilms Inc., 300 North Zeeb Road, Ann Arbor, Michigan 48106-1346.

LC 85-644753   ISSN 0194-3081   ISBN 0-7879-9983-0

NEW DIRECTIONS FOR COMMUNITY COLLEGES is part of The Jossey-Bass Higher and Adult Education Series and is published quarterly by Jossey-Bass Inc., Publishers, 350 Sansome Street, San Francisco, California 94104-1342 (publication number USPS 121-710) in association with the ERIC Clearinghouse for Community Colleges. Second-class postage paid at San Francisco, California, and at additional mailing offices. POST-MASTER: Send address changes to New Directions for Community Colleges, Jossey-Bass Inc., Publishers, 350 Sansome Street, San Francisco, California 94104-1342.

SUBSCRIPTIONS for 1994 cost $49.00 for individuals and $72.00 for institutions, agencies, and libraries.

THE MATERIAL in this publication is based on work sponsored wholly or in part by the Office of Educational Research and Improvement, U.S. Department of Education, under contract number RI-93-00-2003. Its contents do not necessarily reflect the views of the Department, or any other agency of the U.S. Government.

EDITORIAL CORRESPONDENCE should be sent to the Editor-in-Chief, Arthur M. Cohen, at the ERIC Clearinghouse for Community Colleges, University of California, 3051 Moore Hall, 405 Hilgard Avenue, Los Angeles, California 90024-1521.

Cover photograph © Rene Sheret, After Image, Los Angeles, California, 1990.

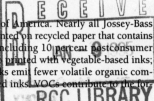

Contents

Editors' Notes

Assessment has become a primary focus of attention at many community colleges, along with such related concepts as accountability, effectiveness, efficiency, productivity, student outcomes, and quality improvement. Assessment is a valuable and necessary endeavor, indeed an essential endeavor, but in reality, it is often a confusing, expensive undertaking that may or may not contribute to the overall improvement or effectiveness of an institution. This *New Directions for Community Colleges* issue contains articles that address the *realpolitik* of assessment from a variety of perspectives, including state-level coordinating boards, accreditation agencies, college presidents, and institutional administrators in a number of different roles. The intent of the issue is to go beyond—some would say beneath—the nearly automatic response that assessment is good and to examine assessment's possible shortcomings and threats as well as benefits.

We begin with a chapter by Virginia McMillan, deputy director for research and planning at the Illinois Community College Board, who focuses on assessment from the state perspective. She identifies pertinent constituencies that interact with state-level community college governance and coordinating bodies; data and information needed for and used with these constituencies; balancing potentially conflicting pressures and ideas about institutional autonomy and state uniformity and control as related to assessment; and mechanisms for presenting assessment data and information so they are accurate, comprehensible, and useful.

Stephen Spangehl, associate director of the Commission on Institutions of Higher Education, North Central Association of Colleges and Schools, acknowledges that assessment is often perceived as a costly ordeal with minimal benefits to the institution beyond meeting external reporting requirements. In his thought-provoking and practical chapter, he presents numerous examples of assessment data already available virtually everywhere, and ways in which colleges can leverage the results of assessment to serve multiple purposes.

Presenting a national overview, Jeffrey Seybert reminds us that although assessment is a global phenomenon, there is great variance in the extent to which assessment is seriously undertaken at institutions, faculty are involved, support systems for assessment are in place, student achievements and learning are actually measured and understood, and results are used.

In our chapter on assessment and transfer, we examine two phenomena that occur regularly in higher education but are virtually never brought into focus together: student mobility, or transfer, and assessment. The fact that students routinely attend multiple institutions before earning a bachelor's or even an associate degree, and are therefore subjected to multiple assessment practices and regulations, imposes a little-explored but growing burden on students and institutions alike. We offer a glimpse into these burdens and some recommendations for institutional collaboration that can ameliorate them somewhat.

Richard Fonte, a president actively involved in planning and leading assessment activities at his campus, argues that presidents can no longer afford to sit passively while others set the assessment agenda. In particular, Fonte addresses the potential conflicts between assessing for effectiveness, for efficiency, and for improvement, and he stresses the central role of research and adequate computer software for implementing high-quality assessment programs.

Involving students in assessment is both essential and challenging. In Chapter Six, Betty Duvall describes a variety of incentives that can encourage students to participate in assessment and to take it seriously. Two of the most important motivations are providing feedback to participants and institutionalizing assessment so that it is not perceived as separate and distinct from regular processes at the institution.

Two of the major changes affecting community colleges over the past decade are the increased diversity of student populations and the need for increased sensitivity to differing norms and expectations of new student groups. Scott Kerlin and Patricia Britz discuss how assessment practices and materials can inadvertently disadvantage nonnative and minority students. They present recommendations for achieving assessment practices that are nondiscriminatory and reduce the likelihood of obtaining misleading, if not false, information about these students' abilities and goals.

Most assessment efforts appear to use quantitative research techniques. In our chapter about qualitative research, we describe several projects that provided rich insights into student and staff experiences and, used in concert with quantitative research, resulted in a more comprehensive and realistic assessment of student outcomes as well as improved programs and services.

In Chapter Nine, Joseph Prus and Reid Johnson present an eminently practical and comprehensive overview of various assessment methodologies, including those routinely as well as rarely practiced at community colleges. They do not advocate all approaches—on the contrary, they suggest that some ought to be soundly rejected because of poor fit with the institution or assessment purposes. For novice as well as seasoned assessment professionals, their work is a valuable guide.

In Chapter Ten, Elizabeth Foote provides an overview of current materials in the ERIC data base on assessment methods, student outcome studies, and the use of assessment as a planning tool.

Trudy H. Bers
Mary L. Mittler
Editors

TRUDY H. BERS *is senior director of research, curriculum, and planning at Oakton Community College, Des Plaines, Illinois.*

MARY L. MITTLER *is assistant vice president for educational services and dean at Oakton Community College, Des Plaines, Illinois.*

Assessment and accountability have become virtually synonymous for state-level decision makers; multiple constituencies for assessment information and the imposition of state-level reporting requirements complicate the assessment environment.

Assessment from the State Perspective

Virginia K. McMillan

The July 1992 *Report of the Task Force on Assessing the National Goal Relating to Postsecondary Education* that calls for the development of a national sample-based postsecondary assessment system exemplifies the increasing emphasis that has been placed on assessment over the past ten years. This emphasis has come from the educational community as well as from external constituents and has resulted in the term *assessment* taking on multiple definitions.

In essence, the assessment movement has become synonymous with the accountability movement. It calls for higher education to examine itself from every possible angle and to share the results of this examination with its consumers. Colleges are expected to assess student skills on entry, assess student progress toward meeting their goals, assess the outcomes of educational experiences on exit and beyond, assess educational programs from a variety of perspectives (cost, quality, need), assess institutional effectiveness in terms of all of the above elements, and assess whether the institution is operating in the most productive manner possible. All these types of assessments are important and interrelated. They make up the components of what Ewell and Jones (1991) call the "New Accountability."

Because of the newer, more comprehensive nature of assessment, there are surely those in higher education who wonder if the term has not taken on one of *Webster's* first four definitions of *assessment* (to tax or fine) rather than the fifth definition (to evaluate). However, whether one defines assessment in its narrower sense or its broader sense, the ultimate goal of any type of assessment is, of course, to bring about improvement. Critics of the current assessment movement say that all too often, state-mandated assessment results are not being used as a mechanism for improvement (Wiggins, 1991).

NEW DIRECTIONS FOR COMMUNITY COLLEGES, no. 88, Winter 1994 © Jossey-Bass Publishers

According to the latest information, more than forty states are involved in some type of accountability (assessment) initiative. Some states have implemented programs based on legislative mandates whereas others have undertaken such initiatives because of state board actions. What has prompted those state-level governing and coordinating bodies to undertake such nonlegislated initiatives? How is assessment viewed by pertinent constituencies that interact with these bodies? What data and information are needed for and used with these constituencies? What is the point of balance between potentially conflicting pressures and ideas about institutional autonomy and state uniformity and control as related to assessment? What mechanisms are in place for presenting assessment data and information so that they are accurate, comprehensible, and useful? These questions will be addressed in this chapter. Assessment will be defined in its broader sense of measuring the degree to which a college or system of colleges meets expectations both in terms of student learning and resource allocation.

Why State Assessment Initiatives?

Only about one-fifth of the states have legislatively mandated assessment, whether it be as student testing or institutional effectiveness. Thus, most state initiatives have been prompted by the actions of statewide coordinating and governing boards. Many of these board initiatives stem from a desire to positively influence change by questioning colleges about student learning, establishing policies, and providing incentives for improvement. These boards also have been sensitive to pressure or potential pressure from legislatures, the business community, and the public. This pressure stems from several nationally recognized reports published in the mid 1980s on the condition of education. Thus, the boards also are using the initiatives to monitor the effectiveness of higher education and communicate the results to constituencies. The general philosophy behind board initiatives has been that it is better for higher education to monitor itself than to be regulated by others who are sincere but may not have the depth of understanding needed to effectively determine how and what to assess. A good example of the latter was the occupational disclosure legislation, forerunner of the current federal Student Right to Know legislation, which required community colleges and proprietary institutions to disclose programmatic graduation and placement rates for all students enrolled in occupational programs. This legislation, though well-intended and on the surface sounding reasonable, failed to consider the wide variation in student clientele served by community colleges as well as the inadequacy of data bases needed to supply such information. Because of the unrealistic nature of the legislation, it was rescinded by the Student Right to Know and Campus Security Act.

On the state level, different approaches have been taken to assessment and accountability—some are more permissive, allowing institutions to determine what measures they will use, whereas others have mandated specific measures.

Still others have combined these two approaches, specifying some measures for which aggregate data are needed at the state level and leaving it to the discretion of the institutions to define other measures that reflect the uniqueness of their institutions.

How Is Assessment Viewed by Pertinent Constituencies?

Constituency groups for community colleges can be defined as internal groups, such as state higher education boards, federal educational groups, faculty, administrators, students, or accrediting associations; or as external groups, such as state and federal legislative bodies, organized citizen groups, business and industry, the media, or the public.

Each of these groups has become increasingly cognizant of the need for better information on what colleges are doing and how well they are doing it. Despite the actions of groups such as the National Education Goals Panel, most of the external groups are not pushing for widespread uniform testing as a mechanism for assessment. Rather, they are asking questions such as How many students are completing their programs of study (graduation rates)? How long does it take them to complete the programs? How many students transfer and how do they perform after transferring? How many graduates get jobs and how well do they perform these jobs? How much does it cost to educate a student and are colleges operating in the most efficient and productive manner possible?

These are not new questions. Until recently, however, inquirers were satisfied with the standard response of "That is a good question, but," followed by a lengthy discourse on the complexity of community colleges and their missions and why there is no answer to the question. At the end of the discourse the inquirer had either forgotten the question, was totally confused, or, in rare instances, understood the difficulty in answering the question. These types of answers are no longer accepted by external constituencies.

State boards have become the entities to which these groups, both internal and external, are turning for answers to their questions. They are, in fact, the logical sources of information about the colleges they coordinate or govern. They serve as the mechanism for disbursement of state dollars and, as such, have a responsibility to be accountable to state legislatures who appropriate the funds and to the general public whose taxes generate the funds.

How Can We Balance Institutional Autonomy and State Control?

For many years, a hallmark of higher education has been the autonomous nature of its institutions. This certainly has been a paramount characteristic of community colleges, where autonomy is embodied in the very name *community*.

In the minds of some, the assessment and accountability movement has come as close as any movement in the past ten years to infringing on local autonomy. Most of the states that have taken the permissive approach to assessment have allowed colleges to define their own assessment measures. This approach can provide incentives for assessment results. However, it cannot easily address the need to uniformly monitor and relay to external constituents the effectiveness of a system of institutions. The latter can more effectively be accomplished by clearly defining a set of measures that can be used across the system. This approach also has the added advantage of providing comparative information to provide benchmarks for institutions to use in conducting their own institutional effectiveness evaluations. It should be understood that this approach does not necessarily impede local autonomy. Academic decisions can still be institutionally based under this approach, and the establishment of statewide measures does not and should not prohibit colleges from using additional measures to assess the effectiveness of accomplishing their individual missions.

What Data and Information Are Needed?

It is critical for state boards to fight the tendency to be either too limited or too inclusive in their approach to defining what will be examined at the state level, for part of the issue between local autonomy and state uniformity and control is more a question of practicality than philosophy. If boards are too limited in their approach, focusing on isolated measures, the results can be misleading. On the other hand, if they attempt to go beyond the limits of what is actually needed, they run the risk of placing unrealistic demands on the institutions. It is imperative to examine the following questions: When do the demands of the state become such a burden that they are detrimental to the goals of assessment? When does responsible leadership by the state turn into a bureaucratic exercise? At what point does a college spend more resources responding to external demands than improving or even practicing its teaching and learning role? In other words, what data and information should be supplied to the state to assist it in fulfilling its role as a motivator, monitor, and/or provider of information?

Two basic types of information are needed. The first can be described as instructional information, pertaining to both students and programs. The second type can be labeled institutional information, looking at how efficiently and effectively the institution performs. Although there is some overlap between the indicators used to measure the performance of these groupings, most information requests fall into these two areas.

Within the instructional area, assessment indicators can be grouped into those pertaining to student achievement and those pertaining to programmatic results. Student achievement measures include such indicators as student goal attainment. This may be the most important and, perhaps, the most challenging outcomes indicator for community colleges. It has long been recognized within the community college sector that students enroll for a multitude of reasons. Unlike senior colleges and universities, where the majority of undergraduates are seeking degrees, this is only one of many objectives for those attending community colleges. For example, in Illinois at least one-third of the student population is enrolled in adult basic, adult secondary, or continuing education. Additionally, many students are taking only selected courses to meet their own needs, such as job preparation where a degree or certificate is not required or to transfer credits to other institutions. In fact, an increasing number of community college students already have baccalaureate, masters, or even doctoral degrees. To use traditional measures, such as graduate rates, for these groups of students is unrealistic. It is therefore critical to develop mechanisms for determining what the goals of students are and for measuring how successful they have been in achieving these goals.

Data on what happens to graduates is becoming increasingly important in assessing the effectiveness of higher education. Information on job placement and how one applies the skills obtained through his or her educational experience, as well as whether students pursue additional education and how well they perform at subsequent levels of education, are all critical pieces of the puzzle. Some of these pieces of information are easier to obtain than others. Uniform follow-up studies are one source of such information. These are becoming more common as standardized follow-up is conducted for state-level studies. Such studies, however, can be expensive particularly if conducted on a census basis. More states are pursuing other sources, such as state wage records and shared college and university data bases, to obtain the basic quantitative data. More substantive data must be obtained through other mechanisms.

State-level institutional measures can include indicators of diversity, cost and revenues, staffing ratios, accreditation results, and examination of infrastructure. In large-population states, it may be necessary to examine many of these factors on a peer group basis, where colleges are grouped by characteristics such as size, relative wealth, and geographic location.

It is important that the primary measurement of both instructional and institutional effectiveness remain at the local institutional level through mechanisms such as program review. It is not feasible or desirable for state-level analysis to go beyond reasonable limits needed for policy-making.

Whatever measures are selected for state-level analysis must be defined clearly so that data are comparable between institutions. For example, it has little meaning to report transfer rates for colleges across the state if the rates are not based on the same method of calculation. Even minor discrepancies in the definition of the cohort groups can result in major differences in results. Whenever feasible, it is better for measurement calculations to be done by a central source using raw data to ensure that apples are compared with apples. The accuracy of the results is only as good as the accuracy of the data on which the results are based.

Presentation of Data

How the data are presented can be as important as the actual data. Much controversy surrounds how to best present statewide assessment data and information so that they are accurate, comprehensible, and useful. Some states have adopted a report card format more commonly used at the K–12 level of education, with each district reporting such items as mean standardized test scores; number of minority, limited-English-speaking, or academically disadvantaged students; and per capita expenditures. Others have taken the approach of presenting the results of assessment on an as-requested basis or as part of statewide policy studies. Cases can be made for each approach. The report card approach provides quick and easy access to the information. Unfortunately, it also increases the danger of misinterpretation and can lead to unfounded conclusions. Assessment measures frequently need more in-depth explanation than the report card format allows.

The piecemeal or more in-depth approach provides for adequate interpretation of the materials being presented and thus affords state-level decision makers the opportunity to establish policies and share data with constituents based on more complete information. A danger of the piecemeal approach is that so many assessment measures are interrelated that key variables may be overlooked if they are not all examined in tandem. This danger, however, is outweighed by the benefits of presentation of information that can more accurately reflect the true condition of education.

Conclusion

There is little doubt that the demands for assessment are increasing and will continue to do so in the future. Those demands have grown beyond the traditional models of assessing student learning into a comprehensive model of evaluating institutions and systems of institutions. Encapsulated in the comprehensive model is assessment of student progress and outcomes as well as programmatic and institutional effectiveness. The goals of this assessment are not only to encourage improvement but also to inform both internal and external constituents of the performance of higher education. In other words, the "A" word has come to mean not only assessment but accountability. State boards are responding to pressures for accountability from legislative mandates or constituency demands by establishing uniform measures of assessment. Few at this point have adopted uniform testing as an assessment measure, although movements are underway at the national level to implement such procedures. Obtaining accurate and consistent data for state-level assessment can be problematic. Improvements in institutional and statewide data bases will be necessary to answer the questions being asked by constituents. Care must be taken in how information is gathered and how it is presented, for it is indeed a powerful tool. In closing, it may be important for educators, whether at the institutional or state level, to ponder the words of Henry Wadsworth Longfellow, "We judge ourselves by what we feel capable of doing, while others judge us by what we have already done." Thus, assessment allows us to let others know what we have done. It is up to us to judge what we are capable of doing.

References

Ewell, P. T., and Jones, D. P. "Assessing and Reporting Student Progress: A Response to the 'New Accountability.'" Denver, Colo.: State Higher Education Executive Officers, July 1991. (ED 337 112)

Task Force on Assessing the National Goal Relating to Postsecondary Education. "Report to the National Education Goals Panel." Washington, D.C.: National Education Goals Panel, July 31, 1992.

Wiggins, G. "Toward One System of Education: Assessing to Improve, Not Merely Audit." Denver, Colo.: Education Commission of the States, 1991.

VIRGINIA K. MCMILLAN is deputy director for research and planning, the Illinois Community College Board.

Many institutions have yet to see the benefits of assessment beyond meeting external agency mandates, but assessment can yield many fruitful benefits, increasing an institution's self-awareness and improving programs and services.

Latent and Leveraged Benefits of Assessment: Expanding the Value of Assessment Information

Stephen D. Spangehl

Assessment is an expensive endeavor, demanding time, attention, energy, and funds from institutions that invariably have other important uses for these resources. Assessment requirements can upset existing schedules, place burdens (real or perceived) on students, and even require the hiring of additional staff. Attempting to measure student academic achievement and the factors that promote it is, for many institutions, an ordeal that seems to yield mostly cost and little benefit.

At accrediting agencies, we have emphasized assessment's function as the R&D arm of higher education, the mechanism by which institutions can discover ways to improve teaching and learning (in contrast to many state governments' stress on comparison of outputs from different institutions). Despite the minuscule portion of their budgets invested in assessment, we still hear many institutions claim that assessment costs more than it is worth.

Not every institution agrees, however. By exploring ways to derive multiple benefits from the information they collect, some colleges have learned to improve the payoff from their assessment efforts. Accomplishing this requires an understanding of the difference between data and information, forethought, imagination, and a willingness to experiment. It also requires an open, systematic, and institutionwide commitment to improving the teaching and learning processes.

Assessment's Costs and Benefits

How can an institution maximize the payoff from its investment in assessment? Broadly, there are two means of improving assessment's cost-benefit ratio: lowering costs or increasing benefits (both can be done simultaneously, of course). In finance, arranging investments to dramatically extend the possibility of high returns is called leveraging, and is a relatively risky practice. Fortunately, in assessment, the risks are minimal and the potential rewards enormous.

Much of the agony over the cost of assessment grows out of misconceptions concerning data. In far too many cases, the desire simply to amass data—particularly when talk of accountability is rife—overwhelms the good sense higher educators usually display. Forgetting any goal for assessment, institutions sometimes try to pile up as much data as they can from as many sources as they can imagine. Thoughts of what to do with the data, what benefits they might produce, are deferred in the panic to get them.

This "datalust" is further distorted by the belief that only precise, numerical data are really informative. Rarely is this the case. Identifying promising approaches to improving teaching and learning is different from predicting which candidate will be elected president or determining the sugar level in a diabetic's blood: accuracy to the third decimal place is unnecessary. On occasion, the need for precision and reliability may determine the choice of method or the size of a sample but, more often than many realize, impressionistic information serves equally well to help an institution identify strengths or problems that deserve further investigation.

This confusion arises because we have intermixed words, using them in ways that cause us to neglect important distinctions in meaning. The term *information* is not synonymous with *data,* which refers to raw observations, perhaps categorized or classified, but otherwise uninterpreted. Nor is information necessarily in the form of numbers, despite the popular tendency to use *number-cruncher* as a name for both computers and researchers (due, perhaps, to one particular strain of data they both seem to relish). Instead, information consists of data used to inform: facts, figures, measurements, and reports that human beings can analyze and understand and use as a basis for deciding on their future actions. Separating the noun *information* from its root verb *inform* distorts its meaning; as long as we stay conscious of the verb inside, we run less risk of thinking about information without the subject and object required conceptually. The subject can be data, but the required object must be a human intelligence seeing the world freshly—*in a different form—* because of the data. Stacked in printouts or bound into reports, survey or test results are inert, valueless data. Digested, understood, and appreciated, those results can inform faculty, staff, and administrators, influencing their actions, policies, hopes, plans, and values.

The volume of data an institution collects and analyzes determines, roughly, the costs of assessment. However, there are often alternative ways to gather particular data, and so costs often vary without affecting the ultimate effectiveness of the assessment being done. To take one example, an institution wanting to gather opinion from alumni on the effectiveness of some particular facet of institutional life might conduct telephone or live interviews, might construct and administer a survey (by telephone or mail), or might use its existing alumni organization and publications to tap the views of its graduates. Cost can vary enormously, from hundreds or thousands of dollars to develop and administer a survey to token expenses for an invitation to comment in the alumni newsletter.

Particularly in today's frugal academic climate, anyone engaged in assessment must think carefully about its potential costs and benefits. Tests, particularly nationally normed ones, are expensive, and even the home-grown variety take time and money to develop, administer, grade, and appraise. Moreover, testing programs must function over time before the results form a pattern worth analyzing. Not only does this increase the overall cost of a testing approach to assessment, but it increases the period before an institution embarking on such a program can expect some tangible return on its investment.

Leveraging the Benefits of Assessment

Both the cost and the use of information ultimately determine assessment's cost-effectiveness. However, estimating the potential benefits of a particular assessment activity is far more difficult than calculating its costs. When someone proposes "let's test all our exiting students" or "let's find out from their employers how well we prepared our graduates," figuring the costs of instrument construction, data collection, and analysis may be complicated, but it is possible. Cost estimates are inevitably on more solid ground than any estimate of what benefits the information collected might produce.

Therefore, a critical juncture in the planning of any assessment activity comes early. When a particular activity is proposed, everyone should be able to envision clearly an act of informing taking place at some time in the future. At the least, this requires pinning down whom the information will inform, when this will happen, and what possible actions, policies, or plans might follow. At a minimum, testing proponents should be able to say with confidence that the departmental curriculum committee will meet for a week in June to analyze and discuss the assessment test results, and that it might consequently propose changing major requirements or the syllabi of particular courses. Assessment schemes that say "results will be forwarded to and analyzed by the appropriate parties" don't promise serious benefits; use of the passive voice, which avoids naming who will do what, emphasizes their lack of focus.

Lending weight to this call to inform, North Central Association of Colleges and Schools (NCA), like other regional accreditors, instructs its visiting evaluation teams and assessment plan review panels to judge assessment efforts on several grounds, such as appropriateness and reality of the implementation timetable, effectiveness of administration, and breadth of the program. A prime criterion is the likelihood that the assessment program will lead to institutional improvement, the weakest aspect of many plans. Of the few writers on assessment who have addressed this problem pointedly, see Alexander W. Astin (1991) *Assessment for Excellence: The Philosophy and Practice of Assessment and Evaluation in Higher Education,* Chapter 7, "Use of Assessment Results."

Extracting the Latent Benefits from Existing Records

Although planning how data will be used after they are collected is critical, there are other ways to magnify assessment payoffs without raising costs. Every institution has mines of data waiting to be turned into useful information. Numerous institutional processes generate records, systematic artifacts of student and faculty behavior. Not long ago, unlocking these fossilized records and making sense of them was a nearly impossible task: when every fact in an institution had to be recorded on paper and filed in cabinets or drawers, less was preserved and what was kept was rarely examined. Today, even with technological advances, there are still too many institutions that have very sketchy impressions of their students' attrition, progress toward graduation, or registration and enrollment patterns—understandings that should naturally emerge from any computerized system for preserving student information. Computerization has made storing, moving, and manipulating data easy; in fact, it is the very ease with which data can be analyzed that is helping make assessment a requirement for all serious educational institutions. Having the capability to store and retrieve data, they now have the obligation to pay attention to them, to draw whatever wisdom they can from them, and to act on the insights they gain. Ignorance may seem blissful, but knowledge demands action.

Some of the ways in which latent benefits can be drawn from these existing records are well-known. Transcripts capture the history of students' studies, successes, and failures; close analysis of course-taking patterns can reveal the strategies we should encourage others to imitate and the ones we should counsel everyone to avoid. Computerized library records may hold similar potential, not for prying into the reading habits of individuals, but rather for seeing whether a group's behavior is affected by various factors. If a general education course, for example, is intended to increase students' appreciation of fiction, students who complete the course ought to read more novels. If business majors check out fewer and fewer books in their discipline, it is worth investigating further what forces may be at work. The trail of records students leave as they negotiate an institution is peppered with other artifacts waiting to be deciphered: student activity records, placement tests, interest inventories, even essays and other answers on admissions applications can all provide useful formative information, particularly when linked with subsequent data on students' actual academic performance.

Using existing records is not the only way to increase the potential benefits of assessment. Often, very modest additions to the data already collected can have quantum effects on the information that can be distilled from them. Academic advising is one of those boundary-crossing institutional activities that illustrates this potential for leveraging assessment benefits. A caveat: this is a composite illustration, built up from aspects of assessment efforts at a variety of different institutions. In my experience, few institutions have engaged in systematic assessment of advising, and none to the extent described here.

Assessing advising offers great potential payoffs, some obvious and immediate, others indirect and more subtle. It is an endeavor about which many otherwise well-informed institutions know very little, an area where relatively inexpensive collection and analysis of data can provide rich information for improvement.

For example, one possibility is to trace back, at the end of a semester, students whose academic performance was unsuccessful because they failed or withdrew from the courses they took. Find out if hours attempted, taken along with other information on how students spend their time, predicts success. (Using the answers it found to this question, Miami-Dade Community College once placed thousands of students on limited load.) See who advised the students who failed, and why they failed despite the advising process. If there is no record of who did the advising, institute one. If advisors cannot remember why they offered the counsel or approval they did, create a means by which future advisors can record such information. It is wasteful to spend as much time and money on advising as most schools do and then to fail to create the artifacts that can be used to determine whether the process is effective.

Sensible as it may be for an institution, suggesting that advising be evaluated will threaten people. Finding out who gives bad advice to students may be in the institution's interest, but it may not be in every individual's interest, particularly if no one has been previously held accountable for advice given. To assess advising well, however, an institution must be fair: it must not assume that advising is a one-sided activity where faculty or staff tell students what to take. Everyone who has advised knows that some students arrive with their minds made up, and no amount of caution or logic can dissuade them from a disastrous course of study. Advisors may not be the problem. However, there are ways to collect data to inform this situation: ask both advisors and students to evaluate each advising session, noting the subjects discussed, the time spent, and the advice offered but refused. Often, students and advisors have remarkably different perspectives on advising: students complain "she never asked me about my career plans" and advisors lament "he seemed interested only in the time and days he could fit courses in, not in what the courses taught." Both perceptions may be right, or both may be inaccurate; without assessment, policy remains founded on hunches.

One thing is certain: assessing advising activities is critical if the process is to benefit both students and the institution. Without such assessment, some may be tempted to follow the dubious lead of institutions that have made advising optional: if students don't want advice, let them do what they want. What incredible irresponsibility! Imagine a physician offering a patient a pen and prescription pad, saying, "if you don't like my diagnosis, take whatever drugs you like."

Assessing advising can have surprising payoffs. For example, consider a problem virtually every community and four-year college shares: faculty constantly complain that new students are unprepared to do the work the faculty expect of them. To find out what caused this perception and whether it was accurate, Elizabethtown (Kentucky) Community College (ECC) examined many things, including the advising system that placed unprepared students in courses they could not handle. (Although other institutions may use this process, I first learned of it at ECC.) Observation of advising sessions made it quickly apparent that advisors had only half of the information they needed to do their jobs. Entrance test results and high school records provided advisors with a fair picture of the skills of entering students, but a correspondingly objective sense of what instructors required of students remained buried in instructors' heads. Consequently, sincere advisors might recommend that students take remedial reading, but ignorantly permit them to take other courses simultaneously where their reading deficiencies preclude any chance of success. Sometimes this happened because advisors just did not know what courses required, and had to guess from numbers and titles.

To get more information about course expectations, ECC did systematic assessment, collecting information from faculty rather than students. Every instructor of a course enrolling first-year students received a form asking exactly what his or her expectations were: How much and under what conditions would they expect students to write or speak in this course? Did they expect students to know how to use the library or write APA-style footnotes? Could they provide examples of particular subject background they assumed students brought with them to class? The survey also asked instructors to photocopy a page from their course textbook and to return it with the questionnaire; these were used to compute readability grade levels for each textbook.

Readability is a simplistic but useful measure of the syntactic difficulty and vocabulary complexity one may encounter in reading, computed by counting the sentences and syllables in a piece of text. Using public domain computer programs and a scanner, it can be measured quickly, with minimal cost. Free programs are available via ftp on the Internet from a variety of sources, such as Simtel20. Another common source is Public Domain Software (phone number: 800-426-3475) in Indianapolis, which has several programs available for around $5.00 per disk (including *Readability Plus* and *Style Checkers*).

Analysis of these readability studies showed exactly what one might expect: expectations among instructors varied widely, and mismatching of student skills and instructor expectations was common. However, using this information for improvement presented challenges. The prospect of asking faculty to revise their courses or change their textbooks held little attraction because it was the faculty who were complaining in the first place about how poorly prepared their students were. Besides, everyone reasoned, faculty would claim an incursion on academic freedom if they were asked to teach *to* rather than *above* their audience. After much discussion, ECC decided to use the data collected to inform the advising process, the place where these student–faculty mismatches started. They produced a book, given to every advisor, containing a page for every course first-year students could take. When students told advisors "I'd like to take Abnormal Psych" advisors could look it up and let the students see exactly what the instructor expected. Students could even do it themselves.

Institutionalizing a system such as this has profound effects. It changes the relationship between students and advisors, giving both the information that helps them focus on what the student needs rather than what the student wants. Publicity puts pressure on faculty with unrealistically low or high expectations. At ECC, before they ordered a text, faculty members began to ask the Learning Center to calculate its readability level. The system arms students with the information they need to make intelligent decisions, helping them understand why "let me give the course a try anyway" isn't a strategy for success. Most importantly, it shows everyone—administrators, faculty, and students—how collecting the right information and sharing it in an effective way can dramatically improve both teaching and learning.

Defining clearly the expectations of faculty for first-year courses can have numerous other effects. Because faculty teaching first-year courses are the "users" of students who emerge from remedial and developmental programs, clearer expectations will work their way down to the remedial level. Remedial programs must help their students learn to do what first-year course faculty expect. Without clear information, their task is hopeless. Assessment provides information.

From this point, it is easy to see how this assessment pattern can spread, how clarity in course expectations and goals for students can ripple through an institution, affecting programs far from its origin. Just as remedial programs should be the foundation for first-year courses, the general education core should be the basis on which students' ability to succeed in more advanced courses rests. If completing the core is, in reality or in perception, irrelevant to success in other courses—one symptom is that students learn from older students to defer taking requirements until later in their academic careers—the core must be changed. Again, to be effective, a general education program must know what others want in students emerging from general education. Assessment can help provide that information, not just here, but also within majors, where advanced courses build on introductory ones.

One final possibility illustrates just how far the ripples might spread, with a little imagination. Thus far, assessment has done little to confront issues of student effort, motivation, and time-on-task, critical factors in student success emphasized by Ted Marchese in his keynote address to the 1993 American Association for Higher Education Assessment Forum. Improving instruction alone does not necessarily improve learning; students have a major responsibility for the process. However, surveys consistently indicate that many full-time college students spend as little as six to ten hours per week outside class studying, while watching television twenty hours a week is typical. Evidence indicates that use of the library is minimal, and use of it as a library rather than a study hall is lower. Lone instructors may attempt to fight these trends by demanding more of their students, but such campaigns, mounted individually, soon turn to retreats. Like grade inflation, "study deflation" is a powerful tide to oppose.

Suppose, however, that every instructor were asked, while listing his or her other expectations for students on the first-year course survey described earlier, to indicate expectations for student study: the number of minutes or hours per week students were expected to spend reading the text, reviewing class notes, writing papers, doing problems, completing outside readings, memorizing, or even thinking. Putting these numbers down in concrete form might far better communicate our expectations to students, and comparing them would undoubtedly be therapeutic for faculty. Adding a simple question to student course evaluations ("How accurate were the published work expectations for this course?") could complete the circle and provide the stimulus for a campuswide examination of expectations that could only improve student learning.

Information Sharing

This discussion of the latent benefits of assessing advising illustrates an important fact about assessment: the need for sharing both activities and results. One extremely effective way to promote this sharing is for every institution to publish an internal fact book that provides all faculty, staff, and administrators with a realistic, up-to-date picture of the institution. A first edition can be built from demographic information: facts about students, faculty, and staff (number, status, sex, age, and race); about programs (enrollment, faculty, budget, space, schedule); and about any other important subject on which accurate information already exists. To be effective, data must be presented clearly and accurately; charts and graphs are helpful, and simplicity is essential. Everyone must get a copy: the object is to communicate the big picture to all, indicating, where appropriate, sources where more details are available.

A fact book serves two important purposes. First, it provides everyone with a common image of the institution as the basis for discussion and planning, hopefully eliminating fruitless academic debates that hinge on differing estimates of the average age of students or the current attrition rate. Second, it sets the agenda for discussion. If it includes (as many do) classroom use data, it will stimulate thinking about scheduling patterns. If it includes distributions of letter grades awarded, it will start faculty talking about the meaning and use of grades. It will generate serious self-examination of academic expectations if it includes the number of hours students say they study out of class, or the number of hours faculty say they want students to study, or both. As additional information is collected through assessment, it can be added to the fact book. Adding it will help guarantee that new data receive attention and that new data are always examined in light of the broader institutional context that gives them meaning.

Another useful mechanism for communicating assessment information is a log of reports, a brief monthly summary of studies and reports completed anywhere in the institution—not the information itself, but the fact that it has been collected and from whom it is available. A useful log should note for whom any study or report was done, what data were collected or tabulated, and who has already analyzed the data; it should also briefly note any conclusions or applications. Logs should include not just internal reports and studies, but also those requested by and submitted to outside agencies. If complete, the log can give everyone in the institution a good picture of the assessment activity underway and establish contacts between departments that would otherwise have little opportunity for communication. It can provide people with existing information that they might otherwise try to collect themselves, and can show people methods that might, in different contexts, help them investigate issues in which they are interested. If expanded to include proposed as well as completed studies, a log can serve as a means of fomenting cooperative efforts and a campuswide approach to assessment.

Ultimately, sharing assessment activities and results among departments greatly increases the payoff from assessment, both by reducing costs and by extracting more benefits from findings. Institutions that earnestly search for ways to leverage the benefits of assessment throb with open discussion of educational goals and methods, the characteristic trait of institutions doing assessment productively. They also discover that support and enthusiasm for assessment develops far more quickly than in an environment where each department tends to its own business. In a vital higher education institution, good teaching and learning are everyone's business.

References

Astin, A. W. *Assessment for Excellence: The Philosophy and Practice of Assessment and Evaluation in Higher Education.* New York: American Council on Education and Macmillan, 1991.

Marchese, T. "Assessment, CQI, and Undergraduate Improvement." Keynote address at the Eighth Annual Assessment Conference and the First Continuous Quality Improvement Conference, American Association for Higher Education, Chicago, June 9, 1993.

STEPHEN D. SPANGEHL *is associate director of the Commission on Institutions of Higher Education, North Central Association of Colleges and Schools.*

Although assessment is a nationwide phenomenon, there is great
variance among community colleges in the extent to which
assessment is occurring, faculty are involved, student
accomplishments are measured, and assessment results
are used for improving programs and services.

Assessment from a National Perspective: Where Are We, Really?

Jeffrey A. Seybert

As is clear from the title, the intent of this chapter is to attempt to provide a comprehensive perspective on assessment in community colleges. I have interpreted this as a charge to deliver a progress report on how far community colleges have come in our efforts to assess student learning and outcomes. It would be interesting, and perhaps useful, to extend this analysis to assessment of institutional effectiveness overall, but such an exercise is outside the scope of this chapter, hence the emphasis on assessment of student outcomes.

Context for Assessment in Community Colleges

Over the last several years, I have spent considerable time reading, writing, speaking, and talking to faculty and administrators in community colleges about assessment. It is from these experiences that I will try to provide this overall perspective. First, however, it is important to briefly set the context for this progress report and to note some of the factors that make assessment of student outcomes a much more difficult task for those in two-year colleges than for those in four-year colleges and universities.

In addition to the barriers faced by all of us in higher education as we try to implement assessment programs, such as faculty resistance, trying to find ways to motivate students to put forth credible effort on assessments of learning outcomes, and the lack of sufficient resources to do the job, community colleges must also deal with some particularly difficult problems. As I have noted on several previous occasions (Seybert, 1990), assessing student outcomes (and, more generally, institutional effectiveness) is especially difficult for

NEW DIRECTIONS FOR COMMUNITY COLLEGES, no. 88, Winter 1994 © Jossey-Bass Publishers

community colleges. We typically have a much broader mission than four-year colleges and universities. In addition to traditional first-year and sophomore-level coursework, community colleges provide career training, occupational retraining, remedial and developmental coursework, community and continuing education programs, courses for special populations, and a variety of other educational offerings. Community college students often are much more diverse in terms of age, background, employment status, preparation, and educational objective than their four-year college or university counterparts (Bean and Metzner, 1985). Thus, student outcome measures commonly used in four-year colleges and universities, such as overall graduation rates and semester-to-semester retention rates, may not be appropriate for community colleges.

Most of us involved in assessment would agree that faculty involvement and buy-in are critical to the success of any effort to assess student outcomes. Thus, factors that would impede or promote faculty participation and support become important considerations in implementation of an outcomes assessment process. There are at least three such factors that I believe warrant brief consideration here. First, everyone involved must understand that assessment cannot be connected in any way to an individual faculty member's performance evaluation. Many faculty, in particular, seem to fear that assessment results will somehow be tied to their individual performance and to salary, promotion, and tenure decisions. It is absolutely critical that very clear and explicit boundaries be set between assessment and performance evaluation and that these boundaries be strictly adhered to. One of the quickest, surest ways to guarantee failure of an assessment effort is the faculty perception, real or imagined, that they will be evaluated based on assessment results. Administrators must make a firm commitment to the absolute dissociation of assessment and performance evaluation.

Second, in general, institution or programmatic assessment should not supplant or compete with assessment in the individual faculty member's classroom, or be imposed without strong faculty involvement. Assessment clearly involves evaluation of overall student learning outcomes, both in general education and at the discipline level. However, evaluation of individual student performance for the purpose of assignment of grades is the sole purview of the faculty member and should take place as a part of course assignments, exercises, papers, and examinations. Individual faculty members may, of course, choose to undertake classroom assessment research projects on their own. It should be clear, however, that the purpose of assessment is evaluation of outcomes at the institutional, departmental, or program levels (assessment of the curriculum and the effectiveness with which it is delivered). As such, it is assessment of neither individual faculty members nor individual students. Of course individual student data must be aggregated at some level as the medium by which assessment analyses are conducted. However, the purpose of these analyses is examination of the institution, its instructional subunits, its curriculum, and the effectiveness of the delivery of that curriculum, rather than of either individual faculty members or students.

Third, assessment is not, if appropriately designed and conducted, an infringement on academic freedom. The principle of academic freedom was established to protect faculty who hold or express political, social, and other views outside accepted or commonly held norms. It should be clear that assessment has no impact on these behaviors. In addition, assessment is not designed to dictate to individual faculty members either what they teach or the instructional methodology they use to do so. This premise that assessment does not infringe on academic freedom is also reinforced by the explicit dissociation of assessment and performance evaluation advocated above.

Finally, the nontraditional attendance and matriculation patterns of many community college students also exacerbate the problems inherent in outcomes assessment. Most of these students attend part-time, may stop-out for one or more semesters during their college career, and may or may not ever earn an associate's degree. Transfer students in particular are notorious for leaving their community college at many points in their careers; in most colleges, very few graduate with an associate's degree before transfer. These circumstances make assessment all the more difficult and give rise to a series of perplexing questions: Which students do we assess? How do we identify them? When should these assessments occur? How long must a student attend a community college before measurable cognitive and affective value can be added? How do we know when to "capture" students for assessment? How do we motivate students to do their best on assessment tasks?

These and other related issues make assessment of student outcomes in community colleges a daunting proposition. It is equally clear, however, that assessment will not go away and that community colleges must address all of these challenges as they attempt to determine the impact they have on their students. Thus, the discussion that follows provides a summary of where we are in terms of assessing student outcomes in two-year colleges.

Outcomes Categories

Student outcomes can be categorized using any of a number of dimensions. However, this discussion will examine three specific ways that a college can affect its students, or, put another way, three types or categories of outcomes. It is useful to frame these as questions.

1. How well did our former students do (and how well are they doing)?
   a. In their community college courses and programs?
   b. As transfer students in four-year colleges and universities?
   c. In their chosen occupation?
2. What and how much did they learn during their community college career (cognitive outcomes)?
   a. In their discipline or major (if appropriate)?
   b. In their general education core?
3. How did they develop, mature, and grow during their community college career (noncognitive, affective outcomes)?

A look at the current state of affairs in each of these categories should provide a reasonable barometer of where community colleges are in terms of their overall progress in assessment of student learning outcomes.

How Well Did Students Do (and How Well Are They Doing)? Clearly, an important set of indices of student outcomes deals with student performance in a variety of areas, both during their community college experiences and after. An entire array of variables, such as historical course and program grading patterns, course retention or attrition rates, performance on professional licensure exams (if available), and, where appropriate, graduation rates, can be collected from college data bases and other records. Similarly, follow-up surveys of former transfer and career program students can yield data regarding the degree to which those students met their community college educational objectives; their evaluations of the quality of instruction, support services, and physical facilities; whether they found a job in the career field for which they were trained (for career program students); their satisfaction with their job or transfer institution; and similar outcomes information. Surveys of employers of career program completers also provide important outcomes data regarding the quality of those students' preparation for work. In addition, data from transfer institutions regarding transfer students' academic performance, progress, and baccalaureate attainment are also significant indices of community college transfer effectiveness.

Finally, there are several ongoing national efforts to define and calculate a national transfer rate by aggregating transfer data from as many individual colleges as possible. These include initiatives by the Center for the Study of Community Colleges at UCLA, the National Effective Transfer Consortium, the National Center for Academic Achievement and Transfer of the American Council on Education, and others (Preston and Bailey, 1993). There is considerable disagreement, however, regarding the details of these transfer rate calculations and many community college research and evaluation experts contend that they seriously underestimate the actual proportion of community college students who go on to four-year colleges and universities. For these reasons, these national transfer rates have not been widely accepted and typically are not used as outcomes indicators by most colleges (although in fairness to their proponents, these rates were generally not intended to be so used).

The degree to which community colleges currently obtain, analyze, and report these data varies widely. In a few cases (California, Texas, Washington, Illinois, and others), the states themselves or some state agency maintains a statewide data base that contains information regarding students who have transferred from that state's public community colleges to its public four-year colleges and universities, although these data may be minimal and may not contain any student academic data (Ahumada, 1993). Similarly, in some cases (Kansas, for example), individual community colleges or groups of colleges have worked out formal data sharing arrangements with some or all of the four-year colleges and universities to which their students transfer in order to facilitate exchange of student academic data. In a few states (such as Oregon), there are analogous statewide arrangements between community colleges and state departments of labor or employment that permit the systematic exchange of data regarding employment of former career program students. Many community colleges are either taking advantage of whatever statewide or regional arrangements are available to collect these types of student outcomes data or are designing and implementing local systems on their own. In addition, some community colleges also survey students who do not re-enroll but also have not completed a career program or transferred. The purpose of these surveys is to determine whether these "leavers" have met their educational objective, their reasons for not re-enrolling, and their satisfaction with their college experiences.

Thus, there is considerable assessment activity of this type underway in two-year colleges all over the country. Clearly, the experience and expertise are available to enable community colleges to answer the "How did our students do and how are they doing?" question. It is important to note, however, that the resources necessary to undertake comprehensive efforts of this type are not insignificant. Regardless, the appropriate methodologies needed to do so have been reasonably well-refined and are in use in many community colleges.

What and How Much Did Students Learn? The difficulties noted earlier in assessing student outcomes are particularly relevant in a discussion of what students learned during their community college careers. Determination of these cognitive outcomes is especially frustrating given the peripatetic nature of many community college students' matriculation and attendance patterns. For this reason, many community colleges that have implemented systematic efforts to assess student learning have decided to define a specific group of students who have had both significant and sufficient experience in the college to warrant assessment of that learning. Most often, this group turns out to be associate degree recipients, who are usually assessed at some point shortly before graduation. Although there is considerable practical merit in defining the assessment population in this manner, embedded in such a definition is a possible methodological confound at some institutions: community college graduates predominantly represent career and occupational programs. Transfer students may thus be seriously underrepresented, a fact that is readily acknowledged by those using this strategy. The complications presented by attempting to include transfer students in assessments of cognitive outcomes, however, generally preclude their inclusion, at least in the initial phase of such an assessment effort.

A variety of assessment methodologies are available to evaluate student learning, including national standardized tests, locally produced assessment instruments, collection and evaluation of portfolios of student work, capstone courses and experiences, internships in business and industry, and final major projects. These methodologies may be used to assess either general education, knowledge in the major, or both. The degree to which community colleges have adopted these cognitive assessment strategies varies widely, although these types of assessments are not nearly as prevalent as those described earlier with regard to how well former students have done (and are doing). It is interesting to note, however, that assessments of cognitive outcomes have been in place for many years in certain disciplines. In the allied health areas such as nursing, dental hygiene, and respiratory therapy, for example, standardized licensing exams have long been required. Similarly, most commercial art programs have routinely required that their students present portfolios of their work before graduation, and in some cases as an integral part of their job interviewing strategy.

In a manner reminiscent of efforts at the state level to provide tracking data on transfer and career program students, some states have instituted statewide programs to assess learning outcomes, such as the regents exam in Georgia, the "rising junior" exam in Florida, and the college readiness exam in Texas. In addition to responding to assessment mandates, in some cases these tests were also designed for other purposes, including evaluation of the need for remediation and student readiness to perform upper-division coursework. These tests are aimed primarily, if not exclusively, at assessment of general education and it is safe to say that they have met with decidedly mixed reactions from community college faculty and administrators.

It is also true, of course, that numerous individual colleges have implemented systematic efforts to assess cognitive outcomes. Jefferson State Community College in Birmingham, Alabama, for example, has adopted an institutional sampling matrix format using the College Basic Academic Subjects Examination (BASE) to assess general education (Calhoun, 1991). Students who apply for graduation are invited and strongly encouraged to participate in the testing procedure, which involves either a relatively short (forty-minute) multiple-choice battery including items in math, science, social science, English, and three cross-disciplinary reasoning skills, or a writing sample. Scores on the modules are then aggregated to yield an overall institutional profile of general education achievement. Although this process does entail several methodological shortcomings, including the aforementioned underrepresentation of transfer students and a reliance on volunteers, it nonetheless illustrates one of the more complete attempts at the community college level to systematically assess general education outcomes.

In many colleges, assessment of general education is coordinated by a representative faculty group such as an assessment steering committee or task force, or by a central assessment office. Assessment in the major or discipline is more often the responsibility of the individual department or program. In many cases, particularly in career or occupational and remedial or developmental areas, specific mandates for assessment may come from external sources such as Carl Perkins legislation at the state level. Thus, faculty in those departments or areas may be charged with determination of program or departmental outcomes and appropriate assessment methodologies, often with the help of research and evaluation specialists.

Assessment at the discipline level in transfer areas is much more problematic for two-year colleges. Most coursework in transfer majors is taken at the upper-division level. Thus, community college students' exposure to the subject matter in those majors may be limited to one or two courses. For this reason, many community colleges have chosen to limit their assessment in transfer areas to general education, although, as noted earlier, this limitation in itself is a difficult proposition due to the various points at which transfer students leave their community college.

Suffice it to say that although there are substantial and growing efforts to assess cognitive outcomes in two-year colleges, these efforts are not yet at the level of those cited earlier designed to assess how well students do.

How Have Students Grown and Developed? Assessment of noncognitive, affective growth and development of community college students is, by far, the category in which we have made the least progress. In their monumental work on how college affects students, Pascarella and Terenzini (1991) found virtually no research that discussed noncognitive, affective gains in community college students. There simply has been very little work done in this area. The few reports that do describe initial attempts to determine noncognitive outcomes have used relatively unsophisticated methodologies. For example, in its career student follow-up, transfer follow-up, and "leaver" surveys, the Johnson County Community College Office of Institutional Research includes a series of questions that ask former students the degree to which they feel their experiences at the college helped them grow in a variety of areas including self-confidence, value and goal clarification, tolerance for people and ideas, ability to get along with others, time management, and others (Johnson County Community College Office of Institutional Research, 1992a, 1992b). Although students generally report gains in all of these areas, these measures reflect their post hoc self-perceptions and, as such, are somewhat limited in their value as indices of affective development. There are, of course, other possible methodologies to measure potential affective growth in our students, including pre- and posttesting with a variety of standardized personality or attitudinal scales. The fact is, however, that community colleges have found these procedures too expensive and time-consuming to use in any systematic way. This may be an area of assessment that will demand considerable methodological creativity, perhaps including the use of focus groups or similar qualitative techniques on small, representative groups of students.

Summary

One final note: the best student outcomes assessment processes and methodologies in the world are of very little value unless the results are used to improve the curriculum and teaching process. Assessment results must be effectively communicated to faculty and academic administrators and used to produce continuous improvement in teaching and learning. This is not to say that these improvements will be immediate or extraordinary—they generally will not. Such improvements are almost always small and incremental. However, the bottom-line reason for doing any outcomes assessment at all is instructional improvement. Assessment results must be applied to the instructional process for this to occur.

To summarize, then, community colleges face numerous hurdles in their attempts to assess student outcomes which, though not insurmountable, do pose significant difficulties in the implementation of those assessments. The fact that many colleges have overcome those obstacles, at least in regard to certain types of outcomes, is to their credit. However, the fact remains that we still have much work to do, particularly in relation to assessment of both cognitive and noncognitive (affective) outcomes.

References

Ahumada, M. M. "Inter-institutional Articulation and Transfer: The Role of Data Bases and Information Systems." *Community College Journal of Research and Practice,* 1993, *17,* 141–152.

Bean, J. P., and Metzner, B. S. "A Conceptual Model of Nontraditional Student Attrition. *Review of Educational Research,* 1985, *55,* 485–540.

Calhoun, H. D. "Implementing Institutional Effectiveness at Two-Year Colleges." In J. O. Nichols (ed.), *A Practitioner's Handbook for Institutional Effectiveness and Student Outcomes Assessment Implementation.* New York: Agathon Press, 1991.

Johnson County Community College Office of Institutional Research. "Follow-up of Career Program Completers: Class of 1990–1991." Overland Park, Kans.: Johnson County Community College, 1992a. (ED 352 075)

Johnson County Community College Office of Institutional Research. "JCCC Transfer Students: Their Destinations and Achievements." Overland Park, Kans.: Johnson County Community College, 1992b. (ED 360 035)

Pascarella, E. T., and Terenzini, P. T. *How College Affects Students: Findings and Insights from Twenty Years of Research.* San Francisco: Jossey-Bass, 1991.

Preston, D. L., and Bailey, R. R. "How Can We Track Students from Two-Year to Four-Year Institutions?" Paper presented at the annual forum of the Association for Institutional Research, Chicago, May 1993.

Seybert, J. A. "Assessment of College Outcomes: Student Educational Goal Attainment." Paper presented at the annual meeting of the American Educational Research Association, Boston, April 1990. (ED 320 948)

JEFFREY A. SEYBERT *is director of research, evaluation, and instructional development, Johnson County Community College, Overland Park, Kansas.*

The mobility of students brings added complexities to the assessment arena; students are being asked to take tests or participate in assessment activities at multiple institutions with virtually no collaboration among schools.

Assessment and Transfer: Unexamined Complexities

Mary L. Mittler, Trudy H. Bers

In this chapter, we draw together two phenomena in higher education that rarely are considered together, but that are notably connected. One is assessment of academic competency or progress; the other is transfer.

Assessment

The growing importance of assessment and placement testing is evident from even a cursory review of topics covered in recent literature about higher education, in general and specialized conferences sponsored by a host of associations, in criteria for regional and specialized accreditation, in state and federal mandates for data collection and reporting, and in the renewed focus on teaching, learning, and student achievement.

At one time, discussions of assessment and placement testing programs often were met with defensiveness and fear. Today, however, these seem to be giving way to meaningful attempts to establish institutional assessment processes, a particularly challenging effort in community colleges, where there are largely transient student populations, wide ranges of student ability, disparate educational goals among students, and large numbers of adjunct faculty.

In this chapter, we focus on two essential elements of assessment measures that examine academic competence and progress (as compared to assessments of student satisfaction, affective growth, or values). The first element is the product: an action or behavior generated by a student, even if this action or behavior is not intended specifically or directly for assessment. Such a product, be it

New Directions for Community Colleges, no. 88, Winter 1994 © Jossey-Bass Publishers

a completed test, a paper, a speech, a performance, a painting, or some other output, can be assumed to reflect the student's knowledge or skills about a given subject area. In other words, a student must do something.

The second element is the measure taken or value attached to this product by someone other than the student, using prescribed rules impartially applied. By this element we mean the following: does the product reflect academic competency or achievement at a predefined level, according to commonly accepted criteria in that field, without regard to such personal characteristics as the student's gender, ethnicity, or previous education? In other words, someone other than the student renders judgment.

This other person certainly can be, and often is, assisted by technology. A commercial computer adaptive placement test, in which the test-taker interacts only with a machine, still requires human beings at the college or university to make decisions about which tests to use, to install and maintain software and hardware, to determine cutoff scores, and to make a host of other decisions associated with assessment. There is thought behind the means by which measure is taken or value attached to the student's work.

In the case of the student who must generate a product, and the ways that measure is taken or value attached to that product, there are costs. Some are obvious: the time, the staff, and the materials necessary for assessment activities. Not so obvious but just as real are the costs of space, computing resources, staff energy, counseling, and tutoring. A thoughtful, comprehensive assessment and placement program can place a tremendous ongoing strain on institutional resources.

Transfer

If there is any new truism in higher education it is that only a minority of degree recipients take all their courses at a single institution. Consider, for example, these data:

- More than half of first-year college students in the nation attend a community college. Any who wish to receive a bachelor's degree must transfer to at least one other institution.
- Of the 2.1 million individuals who attended a public college or university in Illinois during the period from summer 1983 through spring 1990, 242,000 transferred from a community college to a university, or from a university to a community college (the "reverse transfer"). Even more attended more than one public university, or more than one public community college. Even more of these students attended an independent institution as well as a public one.
- In a recent study sponsored by the Society for Values in Higher Education and funded by the Exxon and Ford Foundations, chief academic officers of major research and regional colleges and universities reported that less than 30 percent of their students completed all work for a degree at their college (Smith, 1993).

• A transcript analysis study of a random sample of 1989–1990 bachelor's degree graduates from six Virginia public universities revealed that 59 percent of the students had attended another college or university in addition to their alma mater (Palmer and Pugh, 1993).

Recently, observers of higher education have begun to use these data and other information to examine the transfer phenomenon (Astin, 1993; Bers, 1992; Cohen, 1993; Eaton, 1993; Pascarella and Terenzini, 1991). Among issues they examine are the ways to calculate transfer rates, the effect of institutional type on student outcomes, and the number of institutions attended on the way toward a bachelor's degree. What is not evident in the literature, however, are attempts to examine assessment challenges present when students transfer.

Hypothetical Students and Assessment and Transfer Issues

We present below descriptions of three hypothetical students to illustrate the complexities of assessing student achievement for individuals who transfer.

Student #1. Entered a regional state university as a first-year student. Earned twenty-five credits over two semesters and six credits during the summer at a local community college, then stopped out of school to work for a year. Re-entered the community college for another thirteen credits, then transferred to a different state university for four semesters, accruing another sixty credits of coursework. Changed majors and transferred to an independent institution for a final thirty credits required for the bachelor's degree and completion of necessary courses in the major. Took writing and math placement tests several times, and standardized general education competency tests at the state university and at the independent college.

Student #2. Entered an independent institution in another area of the country immediately after high school graduation in 1968. Completed two years of work, then dropped out to get married and raise children. Over the next fifteen years, took another nine credits of coursework at several different community colleges. Enrolled as a part-time student in a university-without-walls degree program for adults in 1983, and using a combination of credits for experiential learning and traditional courses, accrued the remaining credits needed for a bachelor's degree in 1993.

Student #3. Entered a community college a year after graduating from high school. Earned sixty college-level credits in a three-year period, then transferred to a flagship state university, completing the remaining sixty-four credits for a degree in four semesters.

Student #3, the textbook community college student, unfortunately represents only a small segment of the transfer population. Although the records of students #1 and #2 may seem exaggerated, they do represent the actual attendance patterns of many college students.

What Are Some Assessment Issues Embedded in These Examples?

One issue is institutional accountability and responsibility, or who should assess for what. Each student has attended at least two colleges, and in some cases it is unclear which institutions should be even theoretically expected to have had an impact on the student's achievements. Because transfer is the dominant attendance pattern of today's college student, restricting assessment only to individuals who complete all their work at a single institution, or even the vast majority of their work at one place, would result in assessing only a fraction of college and university students.

A second issue is what to assess: competency in basic academic skill areas such as writing and math, knowledge and skills theoretically acquired through general education, knowledge and skills in the major, or overarching achievements imputed to college graduates such as good citizenship and critical thinking?

A third issue is timeliness. Student #2 extended her education over twenty-five years, with the lower-division general education component presumably completed twenty-three years before receipt of the bachelor's degree. After what period of time are assessments rendered moot because of time elapsed between the educational experience and the assessment activity?

A fourth issue is difficulties imposed on the student by multiple, if not redundant, assessment requirements. Most evident for student #1, how often can institutions of higher education and other stakeholders reasonably ask students to participate in assessment activities, particularly where these involve time outside of regular class work?

A fifth issue implied is the lack of collaboration among institutions, many of which are not willing to accept assessment results, other than officially transferred course credits, from others. This lack of collaboration, perhaps more frankly defined as a lack of trust, results in the demand for both students and institutions to repeat assessment exercises. As noted above, the costs of such redundant measures and programs is enormous.

Suggestions

Assessing student outcomes presumes that the institution has had an effect on the student. As Pascarella and Terenzini (1991) are careful to note, however, changes that occur in a student while he or she is in college are not necessarily the same thing as changes that occur *because* of college. A host of factors outside the college experience per se can influence students, especially students attending school on a part-time basis who spend most of their time in a noncollegiate environment, at work and at home, and whose primary responsibilities are job or family.

The real challenge then, is not whether to assess, but when to assess and how often. Because this challenge can be addressed in a variety of ways, our intent is not to recommend a single solution, but to alert readers to approaches that can be explored. The unique situation of each college will shape which ones make most sense; for example, where nearly all students who transfer move to only one or two institutions, collaborative assessment approaches should be easier to negotiate than at those colleges from which students transfer to dozens of other schools.

With this in mind, to stimulate what we hope might be productive discussions about this issue, we suggest the following three approaches for resolving issues of assessing transfer students:

- Adopt statewide assessment tests and develop statewide data bases so that test results for a given student are accepted and available to all institutions—at least public ones—in the state.
- Faculty from institutions that exchange large numbers of students should work together either to adopt the same assessment instruments or to accept results of one institution's activities as equivalent to their own.
- Reevaluate the necessity for gathering data for its own sake. It takes extraordinary courage to admit that although it may be interesting to know what the reading, writing, and math scores are for transfer students who have completed thirty hours of credit or more at other institutions, it probably isn't of critical importance to them or to the institution. Perhaps a periodic assessment of an entering cohort, regardless of the numbers of credits earned elsewhere, would provide useful comparative data and at the same time ease the burden of administering, scoring, and analyzing such data semester after semester.

In July 1993, the National Education Goals Panel approved a policy to recommend establishment of a national assessment exam to "measure what U.S. college students know" ("U.S. Education Panel . . . ," 1993). Purported at that time to have the ear of the president despite its lack of statutory authority, the panel claimed that its proposed test would be used to set standards for colleges, not to evaluate individual students or compare institutions with each other. Vigorous debate ensued over the appropriateness and utility of a national examination. Among the most immediate, tangible results of Goal 5.5 were a federally sponsored workshop on implementing a national test of student achievements and a thoughtful preliminary study of the feasibility of using measures of good practice as indicators of the quality and effectiveness of undergraduate education as proxies for a standardized, national examination (Ewell, Lovell, Dressler, and Jones, 1993; Pike, 1994). As of July 1994, federal funds for implementation of the National Education Goals were not available and staff had been disbanded.

The potential silver lining in what most educators seemed to believe was an ill-founded and inappropriate attempt to impose a uniform test was that additional light could be shed on student attendance patterns and the relevance of assessment testing for them and their institutions. Voluntary efforts to address the thorny issues raised by assessing transfer students might thus be fostered. Lest colleges continue to be viewed as largely reactionary institutions, responding to the call for accountability only when forced, we suggest that such efforts begin now.

The need to measure student ability and the growth in the numbers of transfer students each poses problems for our institutions. Unless and until they are considered together, however, an even larger issue will continue to go unaddressed.

References

Astin, A. W. *What Matters in College?: Four Critical Years Revisited.* San Francisco: Jossey-Bass, 1993.

Bers, T. H. "Yet Another Look at Transfer: Oakton Students and Bachelor's Degree Recipients at Illinois Public Universities." Unpublished manuscript, Oakton Community College, Des Plaines, Ill., 1992.

Cohen, A. M. "Analyzing Community College Student Transfer Rates." Paper presented at the annual meeting of the American Educational Research Association, Atlanta, Apr. 14, 1993. (ED 354 940)

Eaton, J. S. (ed.). *Probing the Community College Transfer Function.* Washington, D.C.: National Center for Academic Achievement and Transfer, American Council on Education, 1993.

Ewell, P. T., Lovell, C. D., Dressler, P., and Jones, D. P. "A Preliminary Study of the Feasibility and Utility for National Policy of Instructional 'Good Practice' Indicators in Undergraduate Education." Boulder, Colo.: National Center for Higher Education Management Systems, 1993.

Palmer, J. C., and Pugh, M. B. "The Community College Contribution to the Education of Bachelor's Degree Graduates: A Case Study in Virginia." In J. S. Eaton (ed.), *Probing the Community College Transfer Function.* Washington, D.C.: National Center for Academic Achievement and Transfer, American Council on Education, 1993.

Pascarella, E. T., and Terenzini, P. T. *How College Affects Students: Findings and Insights from Twenty Years of Research.* San Francisco: Jossey-Bass, 1991.

Pike, G. R. "The Relationship Between Self Reports of College Experiences and Achievement-Test Scores." Columbia: University of Missouri, 1994.

Smith, V. B. "Phantom Students: Student Mobility and General Education." *AAHE Bulletin,* June 1993, pp. 7, 10–13.

"U.S. Education Panel Plans a College Exam to Establish Standard." *Wall Street Journal,* July 28, 1993.

MARY L. MITTLER *is assistant vice president for educational services and dean at Oakton Community College, Des Plaines, Illinois.*

TRUDY H. BERS *is senior director of research, curriculum, and planning at Oakton Community College, Des Plaines, Illinois.*

Because a president is ultimately accountable for assessment of an institution's effectiveness and efficiency, he or she should play a proactive role in mobilizing institutional resources for assessment; balancing the apparent conflicts between assessing for effectiveness, for efficiency, and for improvement; and communicating assessment results to various constituencies.

Assessment from the President's Perspective

Richard Fonte

A community college president is held accountable for the assessment of a college's effectiveness and for the maintenance and enhancement of institutional quality. This assessment of institutional effectiveness involves, in the words of Peter Ewell (1983, p. 7), a "comparison of results achieved to goals intended," a comparison of institutional performance to institutional purpose.

Calls for Accountability

The call for accountability comes from sources both internal and external to the institution. Interest in the success of any college and the achievement levels of its student body is shared by many parties. Proof of institutional effectiveness is sought by the internal community of faculty and staff and by external entities such as accreditation bodies, state government officials, legislators, taxpayers, parents, current and prospective students, and often a local board of trustees.

The multiple missions carried out by most community colleges further complicate institutional accountability and the assessment of effectiveness. The measurement of student achievement at an academic institution that recognizes the validity of various student outcomes requires sophisticated accountability and assessment criteria.

Assessment provides the information that supports the accountability process. Without assessment feedback, improvement is not possible. The diverse institutional and student outcomes demanded by internal and external constituencies and necessitated by the various missions of the community college should encourage variety rather than uniformity in assessment approaches. Consequently, a president's perspective on assessment as a vehicle for evaluating community college effectiveness, improving quality, and meeting accountability standards is most appropriately developed within a broad framework.

Role of the College President

Although the college president can influence the assessment process, some presidents have chosen to not become actively involved. They risk having external agencies define an institution's effectiveness purely by analyzing disconnected data rather than being presented with a systematic incorporation of quantitative and qualitative measures that might also facilitate institutional change. This is but one argument that can be advanced to suggest that presidents should adopt a proactive approach to the assessment program developed within their colleges.

Within an environment of shared governance, ideally the president and faculty share a mutual responsibility for institutional effectiveness. There is a basic understanding by the college community that the purpose of assessment is to improve campus instructional and support programs and, therefore, the prospects of individual student success. Program review is a long-accepted practice on campuses. Placement exams for entering students are regular components of community college assessment efforts. Moreover, faculty participate on an ongoing basis in direct evaluation of students through classroom evaluation and grading.

While the faculty actively participates in assessments of this nature, the president should be expected to provide leadership that creates an atmosphere of trust. Such an atmosphere facilitates the use of assessment data, even negative findings, to improve instructional quality and measure student progress. Banta (1991) suggests that proper leadership is necessary to ensure that such revelations are not hidden for fear of reprisals. This fear increases dramatically when external accountability sources are added. As accountability shifts away from the internal college community toward external audiences, the purpose of assessment will often seem (indeed, may often be) other than program improvement and student success. The campus atmosphere of trust so critical to the appropriate use of assessment data can be impaired if the president does not exercise leadership to ensure that external assessment reinforces rather than undermines the internal assessment process. Ewell (1989) has suggested that a compliance mentality toward assessment can develop, with state mandates for assessment viewed as a bureaucratic reporting requirement that is not related to any improvement process.

Efficiency-Effectiveness Conflict

The presidential perspective on assessment data required by external constituencies is greatly affected by the potential conflict between the collection of data to prove institutional efficiency and the generation of data in order to measure institutional effectiveness. Efficiency measures may concentrate on such elements as the cost per unit of measurement (dollars per FTE student, for example) whereas effectiveness measures may focus on the data generated by outcome indicators of student achievement.

Efficiency accountability has long been a major interest of state higher education agencies, state legislatures, news media, the taxpaying public, and local college boards of trustees. Efficiency studies are often linked to funding and budgeting; consequently, assessment activities undertaken to demonstrate efficiency are undertaken often to justify a funding increase or decrease. Thus, even when the president and faculty believe that the primary emphasis should be on effectiveness and the measurement of educational outcomes, an assessment program may indeed need to consider demands for efficiency accountability measures. However, in practice, these two assessment demands need not be as mutually exclusive as they might appear. For instance, one goal of assessment may be to determine whether sufficiently high outcomes are achieved given the financial resources provided. Data may indicate how much the college has spent per FTE, but such data may also reflect the dollars spent per educational outcome, such as transfer, job placement, or awarded degrees.

Accrediting Agencies and Assessment Trends

While recognizing the strong pressure on presidents to concentrate attention on assessment measures that demonstrate institutional efficiency, countervailing forces prompt presidents to also focus on the alternative uses of assessment data. Regional accreditation agencies, in particular, reinforce the use of assessment for college or program improvement. In fact, in recent years regional accrediting agencies have required institutions to submit measures that demonstrate the effectiveness with which the institution is fulfilling its educational mission. In particular, these bodies have made it clear that colleges are expected to assess the achievement of their students.

For example, the North Central Association of Colleges and Schools' (1992) Statement on Assessment and Student Academic Achievement stipulates that student achievement is a critical component in assessing overall institutional effectiveness. The expectation is that institutions document student academic achievement. Although the North Central Association is less prescriptive than some other regional accreditation agencies on the exact methodology to be incorporated into an institutional assessment program, the stated purpose of the assessment must be "to enhance student learning and improve educational programs."

The accreditation agencies also expect that the assessment program extends beyond student academic outcomes to include assessment of all institutional functions from student services to the college library and the administration itself (North Central Association of Colleges and Schools, 1992). This, of course, is in addition to the continuing responsibility to demonstrate proper management of fiscal resources. In almost all of these cases, there has been an increase in the need to supply quantitative measures.

In the past, the kinds of assessment required by accreditation agencies permitted many presidents to invest minimal personal attention in the process. Accreditation self-study assessment efforts were set in motion and completed without significant presidential involvement, though not universally. Now, however, this has changed dramatically.

State and Federal Calls for Assessment

The recent call for effectiveness assessment measures by accreditation agencies has been echoed by calls for such measures by the state and federal government. College presidents recognize the need to be attentive to effectiveness assessment, especially when state funding or federal financial aid are linked to such assessment. However, college presidents are also aware and apprehensive of the ways in which state funding bodies will use such measurement data in the allocation of increasingly scarce educational money.

In addition to state requirements, the U.S. government has also increased its focus on institutional assessment. In particular, legislation and regulations related to Title IV federal financial aid have mandated assessment measures. Such federal legislation and regulations include the Standards of Academic Progress (SOAP) and the Ability to Benefit legislation. The financial aid–related legislation is significant because it covers more than the assessment of student outcomes. Most recently, the passage of Student Right to Know legislation will mandate reporting of program completion rates of full-time students beginning with the fall 1991 cohort. The evaluation of student progress throughout the postsecondary experience is tracked and must include matriculation assessment.

Federal Adult Basic Education, Carl D. Perkins, and the Job Training Partnership Act funds also carry assessment mandates. Institutions must provide data on potential and current students and must also provide outcome data. Moreover, the newly emerging federal workforce development proposals appear to be moving even further in this accountability direction.

Accountability and assessment are now inextricably linked. The federal government has issued guidelines requiring accreditation agencies to mandate extensive outcomes assessment. State agencies stipulate extensive effectiveness reports that often mimic the accreditation criteria. Finally, state agencies are attempting to meet the federal mandate to have a statewide system of standards to comply with the Carl D. Perkins Vocational and Applied Technology Act of 1990.

Dangers of External Calls for Assessment

The danger arises that virtually all institutional assessment may become driven by externally imposed evaluations. Miller (1988) suggests that such evaluations may be treated by the internal college community as ends rather than means to institutional improvement. That is, they may fail to provide the information to the faculty and staff to actually initiate enhancement activities of the learning environment. Without presidential involvement, there is a strong possibility that all the external requests will be seen as fragmented and disconnected.

A president must work to ensure that the external assessment demands are related to the institutional needs for instructional and service improvements to the fullest extent possible. Only the president is in the central position to facilitate such a linkage. Ideally, the president should encourage the development of assessment analyses that simultaneously fulfill multiple external and internal assessment requirements, or for which the collection of data can, at least, be interrelated.

Encouraging Multiple Measures of Effectiveness

Assessment of community college effectiveness must be done in the context of an institution's multiple missions. Recent writings on this subject by the League for Innovation in the Community College and by the Consortium for Institutional Effectiveness and Student Success in the Community College start with this premise. One such publication by Doucette and Hughes (1990) suggests sixty-nine key assessment questions within a framework of four principal instructional missions: transfer, career preparation, basic skills/developmental education and continuing education, and the unique community college mission of access. The Consortium for Institutional Effectiveness and Student Success outlined at the 1993 AACC conference twelve assessment areas as an absolute minimum assessment program. These involve student assessment on entry, during college, at the exit point, and after leaving the college.

The main message provided presidents by the emerging literature on assessment is the importance of multiple measures of institutional effectiveness. Rather than searching for a single indicator to demonstrate success of a community college, presidents must foster a campus climate that recognizes the value and use of many different evaluation benchmarks. Although it may not be surprising to suggest that multiple missions require multiple effectiveness measurements, it is also true that each mission may also need to be looked at from several points of view. Thus, there will be several indicators for each mission.

Developing Institutional Assessment Capabilities

The president must be responsible for ensuring that an adequate assessment capability exists at an institution. There are two major ways this responsibility may be met. First, the president should support the creation of a data processing system that will facilitate the assessment function. Second, there must be presidential support for a research function committed to evaluating institutional effectiveness.

Student Tracking System. The most important data processing issue relating to institutional effectiveness assessment involves the acquisition of mainframe or client-server software necessary to implement a student tracking system. Campus administrators primarily use the data processing mainframe system in conjunction with their respective administrative functions. Therefore, the majority of administrators are not generally focused on institutional effectiveness measures or assessment data when making decisions about new mainframe software. Presidential involvement in key decisions concerning software is essential to ensure that assessment capacity will be expanded by the purchase of any new software or software enhancements.

Without presidential commitment, key data elements essential to establish and maintain a longitudinal tracking system may not be gathered. For example, to adequately determine community college institutional effectiveness with its multiple missions, the determination of student intention is important. Student intent (transfer or occupational) must be recorded at the point of initial registration and for each subsequent registration. Often, admissions and registration personnel may rush students through lines without gathering or updating such essential information.

The critical elements in the student tracking system require the capability to measure outcomes using longitudinal data bases and also the capability to store student-specific assessment data gathered during matriculation and registration. In addition, summary assessment of institutional effectiveness is dependent on student tracking systems that identify areas for program improvement.

Many software packages, such as those that are microcomputer-based, allow an institution to assess student outcomes for a cohort of students. Academic improvement for a particular student, however, may depend on the use of individual assessment data for that student to guide the counseling, advising, registration, or course placement process. A student tracking system focused solely on cohort outcomes would limit a president's ability to create a proactive assessment environment on a campus. The student tracking system must not only track outcomes, but also monitor individual student progress based on particular assessment criteria. Ideal student tracking systems use these assessment criteria to facilitate interventions that will encourage student success. The president needs to provide the resources to establish such a tracking system that addresses both the need for cohort data and the need for individual student data.

Office of Institutional Research. The president has a responsibility to facilitate the analysis and communication of assessment data on campus. Although there may be a variety of approaches to carry out these activities, establishing an office of institutional research will assist the dissemination process to both internal and external constituencies. The institutional research office must become a focal point of the assessment data analysis.

The director of institutional research should not have the sole responsibility for the assessment process, but should help develop and implement a comprehensive, cross-institutional assessment strategy. The office can act as a resource to those on campus seeking to evaluate the effectiveness of a particular institutional program or activity. The director should also serve as an advisor to the president on assessment issues.

Communicating Assessment Information

Presidents understand that not all assessment information is equally wanted by or useful to all the constituencies seeking information about the college. Some data should be gathered primarily for internal audiences, whereas others should address the key requirements made by the community, the local board of trustees, or the state and federal government. In each case, the assessment measure should have a specific function and should yield data that provide a fair representation of the effectiveness and efficiency of a particular institutional mission or function.

Naturally, assessment indicators differ in their degrees of complexity and aggregation. For example, retention information at the institutional level is more relevant in public reports, whereas such information at the program level is more significant for internal use by faculty and staff. Basic market share information by high school or town may be an adequate public measurement of the fulfillment of the access mission, but internal campus analysis may need further breakdowns by senior class rank, placement test results, or the level of math and English preparation. More detailed information may be necessary to provide adequate feedback to initiate an improvement cycle, whereas more general data may provide a measurement or status report on the current situation.

The president must consider the importance of communicating appropriate assessment information to each constituency. Annual effectiveness reports could become an important component of a broader communication strategy. A public accountability report should include benchmark results from mandated state and federal reports, but should be complemented with assessment outcomes that most accurately describe institutional progress on the priority elements of the local community college mission.

For such public reports, the president should pick a limited number of key indicators for each mission of a community college. In all probability, they should address the basic community college functions of transfer, career education, basic skills, remediation, and access. Because such a report would be widely distributed, the mission measurements should be distinctive and able to stand alone. A selected benchmark should not crowd out or overlap another key indicator of another mission. For example, it would be inappropriate to use a transfer rate to assess the transfer mission if such a statistic included all occupational students in the calculation.

Assessment Feedback Loop

In his article on institutional effectiveness, Hudgins (1993) quotes Macomb Community College president Albert L. Lorenzo, who believes that "effectiveness is not a measurement process, but a change process" (p. 44). This statement should be viewed as a proposition that can be tested. Such a proposition may well find itself supported, or not supported, according to the presidential perspective taken on the gathering, analysis, and use of assessment data.

Past thrusts of the assessment efforts were directed more toward accountability than toward improvement. Such assessment activities led primarily to the generation of data used to complete efficiency reports called for by internal and external constituencies. Today, however, it is clear that assessment should be part of a continuous improvement process, incorporating not only efficiency, but also effectiveness measures.

The president has the opportunity to facilitate the use of assessment data to improve the quality of education offered at the college. Although various approaches can be used by presidents seeking to establish a positive change environment, Kreider and colleagues (1993) stressed the link between feedback and the strategic planning process. The nineteen quantitative and qualitative factors in Mt. Hood's program improvement process are used in an annual planning cycle to initiate improvements.

The emphasis on feedback and improvement also provides linkage between the assessment process and total quality management (TQM) or continuous quality improvement (CQI) movement. Chaffee and Sherr (1992) suggest that continuous learning improvement will occur to the extent that assessment focuses on the results of the subprocesses within the instructional process. The internal assessment process traditionally accepted by faculty is closely aligned to TQM principles of data feedback. Friedlander and Mac-Dougall (1990) provide examples of colleges providing feedback through the program review process, among other approaches.

In facilitating the broader use of assessment information, the president is in the position to influence whether improvement assessment or compliance assessment will be the campus emphasis. The presidential perspective toward assessment affects the entire campus change process. If a president takes a reactive rather than proactive posture, responding most enthusiastically to external accountability requests, the internal campus environment will be adversely affected or, at least, other-directed. A program improvement orientation will be facilitated on campus if a president exercises leadership in coordinating the institutional response to both internal and external demands for assessment and accountability.

References

Banta, T. W. "Assessment Update: Ends, Means and Results." In *Proceedings of the Effectiveness and Student Success Second Annual Summer Institute,* 1991.

Chaffee, E. E., and Sherr, L. A. "Quality: Transforming Postsecondary Education." ASHE-ERIC Higher Education Report No. 3. Washington, D.C.: George Washington University, 1993.

Doucette, D., and Hughes, B. *Assessing the Institutional Effectiveness in Community Colleges.* Laguna Hills, Calif.: League for Innovation, 1990. (ED 324 072)

Ewell, P. T. *Information on Student Outcomes: How to Get It and How to Use It.* Boulder, Colo.: National Center for Higher Education Management Systems, 1983. (ED 246 827)

Ewell, P. T. "About Halfway: Assessment at the Balance Point." *Assessment Update,* 1989, *1* (1), 1–2, 4–7.

Friedlander, J., and MacDougall, P. R. "Responding to Mandates for Institutional Effectiveness." In P. R. MacDougall and J. Friedlander (eds.), *Models for Conducting Institutional Research.* New Directions for Community Colleges, no. 72. San Francisco: Jossey-Bass, 1990.

Hudgins, J. L. "Institutional Effectiveness: A Strategy for Renewal." *Community College Journal,* 1993, *63* (5), 41–44.

Kreider, P. E., and others. *Institutional Effectiveness and Student Success.* Gresham, Oreg.: Mount Hood Community College, 1993. (ED 356 843)

Miller, R. I. *Evaluating Major Components of Two-Year Colleges.* Washington, D.C.: College and University Personnel Association, 1988. (ED 301 300)

North Central Association of Colleges and Schools. *A Guide to Self-Study for Commission Evaluation.* Chicago: Commission on Institutions of Higher Education of the North Central Association of Colleges and Schools, 1992.

RICHARD FONTE is president of South Suburban College, South Holland, Illinois.

Motivating students to participate in assessment activities and to take these efforts seriously is a continuing challenge.

Obtaining Student Cooperation for Assessment

Betty Duvall

Pizza just doesn't do it. Baseball caps or T-shirts don't do it. Discounts at the college bookstore don't do it. None of these are likely solutions to the problem of how to get community college students to take assessment tests and to get them to really give it their best.

A recurring problem for many community colleges embarking on an assessment program is how to get students to take the tests. Even with successful student involvement in placement testing, involving students in outcome testing may be even more difficult (Lutz, 1994). Moreover, getting students to not only take the tests but to take them seriously, to be motivated to do their best work, adds to the institution's problem.

Early in the assessment testing movement, institutions tried many different reward systems. One college offered pizza to students as they completed tests. Several colleges, encouraged by national testing services, gave students T-shirts or baseball caps as a reward and as a way of spreading the news that testing was for everyone. One enterprising college even sought to encourage students in testing by offering a substantial bookstore discount on textbooks to students who completed testing. However, institutions interviewed reported that none of these worked as well as needed or hoped. As more colleges move into assessment testing, a major problem continues to be how to get students to take the tests, whether the testing is to determine students' competency level in basic skills in order to place them in course work appropriate to their needs and to lead them to successful academic accomplishment, or to measure the outcomes of their college work.

Community colleges take pride in their open-door policy providing access to all people and all ages. As a consequence, community college students are usually part-time, burdened with jobs, family, and community responsibilities in addition to an academic program. They may rightfully resent the extra time required to take placement tests before registering for classes. As adults, they often resent advice regarding the course they should take. Although many are in identified programs with degree or certificate goals, many may just want a few specific classes related to job improvement and will happily take the chance that they have the necessary basic skills for success in the course.

Once the student has completed a program, whether that program is a full associate degree, certificate, or just student-identified courses to meet individual needs, it is even more likely that the busy student will resent the time required for measurement of outcomes. Students may perceive testing as useful for the institution but of no help to themselves.

Furthermore, how does the college get students to do their best on the test? Can the college get an accurate measure of the students' skills and ability as they enter and exit to measure the value added by the academic experience?

Obtaining Student Participation

Colleges interviewed that have successfully involved students in testing have established assessment testing as an integral part of the institution. Assessment testing has been institutionalized. Those colleges noted that no student ever questions course tests, quizzes, or exams as a part of college work. Many students, perhaps overly grade-oriented, eagerly seek tests and information about testing from the teacher in search of better grades. The same mindset transferred to assessment testing ensures eager student participation and student response at the highest level possible.

Mission

Colleges successful in testing have a well-defined mission and goals statement that includes the purpose of testing. If assessment is to be an integral part of the institution, that must be clearly stated in the mission of the college.

The one basic purpose of assessment testing should be to improve instruction and ensure student success. If students know that the primary goal of testing is to help them be successful, their willingness to participate is greater.

At one college, the statement of mission and the purpose for testing is a prominent part of every college publication, beginning with recruitment materials and continuing on through course schedules to information regarding graduation and leaving requirements. The idea of measurement has been consistently and constantly kept in front of the student, not as an add-on to the instructional program, but as an integrated part of academic work. Assessment is sold to students at the time they are recruited and admitted. Students come to the institution knowing that testing is part of the institution's plan for their success; they know that it is part of the college's goals. If students can take pride in knowing they are attending a college where excellence is planned and where quality is measured and assumed, there is much less student resistance to testing.

Administrative Leadership

Administrative leadership has been an important factor in successful student participation in assessment. At one successful college, the president has set the goal for assessment and has articulated assessment as part of the institutional mission. She has kept the idea of assessment before the entire academic community: faculty, staff, and students. In this community, where the college and community are closely associated, she speaks about assessment at service clubs and other groups to integrate the community expectation of quality assessment in all that the college does. She has supported assessment as part of the maturation of the institution. This effort has not been lost on students or prospective students, and enhances and influences their expectations of the college experience.

Presidents may also want to consider certain extrinsic rewards (other than pizza and T-shirts) for student participation, rewards that highlight and honor student achievement. Examples from successful programs include the following: a luncheon or reception to honor outstanding student achievement in outcome testing has proven motivational to other students; invitations to outstanding students to give short presentations to local community groups and service clubs reflect well on the student and institutional accomplishments and serve to motivate others. Despite the busy schedule of community college students, few are too busy to receive honors. The inclusion of faculty in such events recognizes their participation in student success. Another college waives the add and drop fees if students or teachers find they should be in a lower- or higher-level course. Other extrinsic rewards might include preferential access to registration times, better parking spaces, or bookstore discounts. However, extrinsic rewards alone are not sufficient to achieve student participation or high motivation in testing.

At successful colleges, the chief academic officer and the chief student development officer are strong advocates for testing and work in close partnership in the assessment process. One side of the academic house can undo the work of the other if common understandings and strong relationships are not developed early on. Students will know at once if teaching faculty think assessment is unimportant or if counselors and advisors show no enthusiasm for it. The result will be low student participation or weak motivation.

Curriculum

Assessment as part of a well-defined curriculum is a second important factor. Students must see testing as a part of what normally happens during their academic career. Assessment testing, like course examinations, must be an ongoing process. Courses and testing should be interconnected, should build on

one another, and one should naturally follow the other. If testing is a continuous curriculum process, students are more likely to accept it as a part of normally experienced college work.

This notion is greatly enhanced as students are involved in assessment testing in elementary and high school experiences. Students who have been
assessed as part of their precollege program are far more likely to accept college assessment as part of the curriculum. An additional benefit of assessment
is the link it can provide between the high school experience and college.

Faculty Ownership

Successful colleges have also cultivated a sense of faculty ownership of testing.
Faculty can and will tell students its importance and usefulness if they believe
in its purpose.

Assessment testing can be institutionalized yet not faculty-owned. When
that happens, testing directors report that the program has not been successful and student participation has been difficult to gain. Faculty must help
invent the assessment program; assessment cannot be bought off the shelf by
administrators and a few faculty members. Faculty members are likely to be
apprehensive that student assessment will be based on personnel evaluation.
They are certain to feel insecure if there is any hint that their personal evaluation is related to student outcome assessment. A successful assessment program must provide results that are useful to individual faculty as well as to the
institution as a whole. Faculty must be prepared for the implications of assessment; they may learn some unpleasant things about student learning. If they
know in advance that what is learned from assessment is theirs to use, to
improve the successful academic accomplishments of students, fear and insecurity will be reduced and educational quality increased. Testing directors also
caution that the entire academic community, including classified support staff,
must understand and advocate the purposes of assessment. A short informative statement given to all classified staff has helped at one institution interviewed. A narrative statement that explains the purpose of assessment to the
clerical staff who schedule students for testing is especially crucial.

Student Ownership

Colleges with active testing programs have involved all students in the testing
program; students want to know that this is part of the institution's plan for
everyone, that certain students are not being singled out. Those colleges have let
students know that assessment is expected of every student. They have publi-
cized assessment and given students advance notice of the testing requirement.
Colleges should include testing information in application letters, in the class
schedule (in more than one place), and in the formal application letter for graduation from the registrar. They should tell students that exit assessment is one of
the qualifications for graduation or leaving. Follow up that letter with one from

the president with information on exit assessment. Tell students that the tests will not affect their grades. All staff must be prepared to answer student concerns positively and enthusiastically. Students will complain that this is a busy time of the year, ask what testing has to do with a course, or wonder whether testing is needed to transfer. Staff should be prepared to answer those concerns.

An institution with a long history of assessment testing has found it important to make the testing environment as comfortable, convenient, and pleasant as possible. Their assessment room has good light, comfortable seating, and sufficient table space. They offer coffee and soft drinks and strive to make the testing as time efficient as possible. Most important, successful institutions involve students in a celebration of excellence. They let students cultivate pride in their individual accomplishments and in being part of an institution that demands excellence and produces quality. Student assessment testing participation has become a badge of honor.

Feedback

Community college students in all their diversity have one thing in common: they want to know that they are a part of the college, they want to participate in decisions affecting their academic lives. Students and faculty expect to receive information regarding the results of testing.

Obviously, then, to gain student interest in testing, the institution must spend some time in developing a readiness for assessment. The institution should assess graduating and leaving students at the end of each term. Once students have left the institution, bringing them back for testing is impossible.

Motives will be questioned and assurances needed. Anxiety toward testing, as for any significant institutional change, will be high. Insecurity and misunderstandings take time to overcome, but in the end, it is time well-spent for encouraging student participation.

To provide appropriate information to students and faculty, testing results and analysis must be readily understandable. This is not the time for jargon-filled, hard-to-follow data or rules, one testing director reminds us. Faculty and staff should recognize the many commitments of community college students and not ask them to participate in testing that is not really necessary or for which students or faculty see little purpose. Students do want to participate in celebrations of excellence of themselves and their college. They want to be part of the team providing for the quality assurance of their academic program.

Students want to see that data collected are used to improve and never to punish. If students perceive that faculty or other students reap negative results from testing, there will be little enthusiasm for testing participation.

Faculty needs are similar. There must be full and complete information provided to faculty from assessment. They must own the information and use the results for curricular, pedagogical classroom management decisions. Testing must answer questions that faculty members pose in order to be useful to instructional improvement.

Summary

Motivated student participation in an institution's assessment program can be accomplished. Major factors for success include the following:

A strong sense of institutional purpose for testing should be included in the mission statement and clearly communicated to students. Testing must be an integral part of the institution's academic program, not just an add-on.

Strong, committed support of all levels of administration is essential. The leadership of the president and other administrators must be evident to faculty, staff, and students.

Assessment testing should be integrated into the curriculum, providing a loop that leads to continued review and improvement of the instructional program. Students must see that their testing participation leads to change and improvement.

Both faculty and students must feel a sense of ownership in the testing program; they must see that they influence the continued development of assessment testing and that they reap the benefits that result.

Feedback of testing results is important to student acceptance of the program. More crucial, however, is feedback to students, faculty, and the community of changes (curricular and institutional) that result from the assessment program. Students want to know that they are making a difference; they want to have pride in themselves, their accomplishments, and the institution of which they are a part.

Throughout the assessment process, student participation can be enhanced by both extrinsic and intrinsic rewards, but intrinsic is the most powerful motivator. Students must be brought to the assessment process; they must see that they benefit from it. Students must see assessment as part of the normal everyday activity of the college. They, like faculty and staff, want to see that assessment serves their needs and those of the institution and community.

Reference

Lutz, D. "Motivating Students for Successful Outcomes Assessment." Paper presented at the Sixth Annual Summer Institute on Institutional Effectiveness and Student Success, Atlantic City, N.J., June 19-22, 1994.

BETTY DUVALL is community college liaison to the assistant secretary at the United States Department of Education, Washington, D.C.

The growing diversity of student populations presents community colleges with special assessment challenges.

Assessment and Diversity: Outcome and Climate Measurements

Scott P. Kerlin, Patricia B. Britz

In this chapter, we present an overview of issues that are of particular importance to community colleges concerned with serving the needs of culturally diverse student populations and incorporating these efforts into campus assessment programs. First, we offer an overview of the most important considerations for community college campuses when assessment activities are being developed with the needs of culturally, ethnically, religiously, and linguistically diverse students in mind. Then we describe efforts at North Seattle Community College to address these considerations.

Who Are the "Diverse" Students in Community Colleges?

As postsecondary educational institutions intended to serve local communities, community colleges are called on to meet the range of needs of their various constituents: students, employers, four-year colleges and universities, school districts, and other members of the public. Because of their traditional role as open-door institutions, community college students represent a wider range of local citizens than do the more selective four-year institutions of higher education. Community college student populations represent individuals from most ethnic backgrounds found in the local region, as well as a broad spectrum of ages and incomes. Additionally, community colleges are often called on to serve the educational needs of citizens and immigrants whose native language is not English. In some regions of the United States, English as a second language (ESL) is one of the fastest-growing areas of study in community colleges. Other students with special educational needs, such as those with differential learning abilities (sometimes referred to as the learning disabled), find the community college more accommodating than four-year institutions.

For the purpose of this chapter, we will use the term *diverse students* to refer to a broad array of individuals who are typically underrepresented in four-year institutions. These individuals include people of color, differentially abled, and non-U.S. citizens. However, by discussing assessment activities pertaining to "diverse" students, we do not mean to slight the educational concerns of traditional students (otherwise referred to as white Americans, who still make up the majority of the student body in most of America's community colleges). Rather, we wish to sensitize the reader to the fact that as the student body diversifies, we believe it is unfair and detrimental to all students—as well as to the quality of education—to treat everyone's needs similarly when community colleges seek to enhance their assessment activities to serve the needs of their community constituents.

Because students attend community colleges for a wide variety of purposes, it is not appropriate to expect that most students who enter such institutions will eventually earn either an associate's degree or a vocational certificate. Assessment activities (either campus-based or state-mandated) that focus on such expectations are likely to turn up disappointing evidence that relatively small proportions of community college enrollees complete their programs of study and graduate. Nevertheless, it is very important for campus assessment activities to focus on differences in educational outcomes of their students of color in order to determine whether changes in campus climate or teaching practices are needed.

Assessment Activities That Respect Student Diversity

Although the ethnic and cultural diversity of community college students has changed significantly in many regions during the past two decades, the level of awareness of many campus staff, faculty, and administrators about the educational needs of diverse students sometimes has not kept pace. Indeed, the diversification of students has often far outpaced that of college employees, even in large urban areas with significant populations of people of color. As long as the ethnic or racial backgrounds of students and employees remain significantly different, there is greater potential for misunderstanding in communications between students and college personnel. If not addressed, these misunderstandings may alienate students from participation in classroom discussions as well as from participation in campus activities. In the worst case, students may withdraw altogether from the campus, leaving the institution with a serious retention problem.

Nothing can make as big a difference in changing the culture of the community college as the commitment of its administration, faculty, and staff to change. When college employees are actively engaged in improving the climate of the college to serve the needs of diverse students, students in turn feel a noticeable improvement in interpersonal relations. We believe that ultimately, college administrators and other personnel must be committed to transformation of the campus climate in favor of serving and respecting diversity.

When we talk about campus assessment activities that take diverse students into consideration, we must consider at least two kinds of assessment: classroom-based assessment in individual courses and campuswide assessment. The first kind of assessment pertains to methods of determining levels of knowledge of students as they enter a class and knowledge gained through participation in and completion of the class. Assessment techniques of this kind can take on a number of forms, from traditional written skills examinations using experimental design approaches (pretests at the term's beginning and posttests at the term's end) to a variety of techniques designed to give qualitative, ongoing feedback of student learning. The goal is to improve both learning and instruction during the term rather than by evaluation of students (course grades) and faculty (course evaluations) at the end of the term.

Additional assessment methods at the course level include small group instructional diagnosis (SGID), classroom assessment techniques (CATs), and capstone portfolios in vocational programs. These techniques, coupled with a growing concern for quality of learning, provide a conscious change in awareness of different learning styles and the need to develop corresponding teaching styles to meet different learning needs. However, this presents a growing tension between faculty steeped in traditional teaching models and others with interest in using teaching paradigms that adapt teaching techniques to the learning needs of the diverse students in the classroom.

Assessing learning and the effectiveness of classroom activities for diverse students are even more troublesome to the traditional teacher used to dealing with term course evaluations. Other faculty are discovering assessment techniques that focus on the collection of informal, ongoing, shared (and often anonymous) assessment of student learning in situ, while the class is meeting. If assessment is both systematic and ongoing, it should stimulate immediate changes in how teaching and learning proceed. Faculty making appropriate changes in a less judgmental manner are more tuned to different learning styles and more sensitive to diverse learning needs. The key may be as simple as the inherent anonymity of the assessment process, built into a setting where trust has been demonstrated. The ultimate desired outcome could be students being willing to take more responsibility for their own learning.

Campuswide assessment methods are attempts to determine the impact of the college's teaching and learning activities as well as the learning environment on the quality of learning and the overall educational experiences of students. Campuswide assessment methods seek to determine whether students who enroll in the community college are able to be successful at their self-defined educational endeavors, and if not, to determine the causes of students' failure to meet their goals. Tracking studies, degree and certificate analysis, and other student outcomes can be correlated to enrollment trends to statistically determine students' rates of success or failure and to forward theories about their causes. Additionally, studies can be conducted by college personnel to assess the overall campus climate in order to assess what aspects of the campus have significant effects on student enrollment, retention, and graduation patterns.

When conducting campuswide assessment studies, researchers must look for variations in outcomes on the basis of students' different educational backgrounds as well as differences in ethnic or cultural backgrounds. Not all students learn in the same manner, and not all students come to the community college with the same levels of preparation. In order to assist students with different educational and social needs, campuses should seek information that tells how students differ by ethnicity in such areas as retention, graduation rates, transfer to four-year institutions, and length of enrollment before graduation.

National data studies lend much credence to the observation that student success at both two-year and four-year colleges varies by ethnicity, with Asian-American and white students typically showing higher rates of success than African-Americans, Native Americans, and Hispanics. Campuses must conduct studies of their own students' performance in order to determine whether outcomes are varying by ethnicity and, if so, how to address these variations. Data can be collected and analyzed on a campus-by-campus basis using state data reports on enrollment and graduation to determine how well the campus is performing relative to peer institutions across the state. Data should also be gathered on the departmental and program levels to determine the variations that exist in student outcomes as a factor of ethnicity of enrolled students.

Another level of campus assessment can be conducted by carrying out a campus climate study. Climate studies can be used to assess students' and employees' opinions of the quality of the campus learning environment and social environment in order to identify significant causes of student success or failure on the basis of ethnic or cultural background differences. Much care must be taken in developing and conducting such a study and in presenting the results to the campus community. Done effectively, a campus climate study can significantly heighten awareness across the campus that cultural diversity is an important and valuable asset. However, precisely because it elevates the issues of race relations and ethnic student outcomes on campus, a climate study may also heighten tension across campus when results are released.

In considering the assessment of diverse students at the classroom or campus level, it is essential to recognize that assessment instruments can never be truly neutral or objective in their measurement of learning and other student outcomes. Biases and assumptions about student learning are often introduced in such instruments, based on the expectations and assumptions of the persons designing them. Additionally, biases can be introduced in the process of administering the assessment methods. Biases or assumptions about students' abilities based on ethnicity or racial status will inevitably affect the outcomes of assessment activities and will distort the true findings about students' progress.

Assessment Activities for Diverse Students at North Seattle Community College

Assessment of students' performance and their attitudes toward diversity and multiculturalism have been the subject of research conducted at North Seattle Community College since 1991. In this section, we focus on areas of assessment carried out, findings reported, and implications for further research.

In 1991, North Seattle Community College received a $2.5 million, five-year Title III grant from the U.S. Department of Education. Thanks to this funding, the college developed a new office of institutional research. In its first year of operation, this office was instrumental in carrying out a campuswide multicultural climate study. This study was supported under the Title III grant's multicultural component, which provided funding "to create a climate where cultural diversity is recognized and valued." The focus of this funding was on curriculum change through creation of new multicultural courses as well as infusion of multicultural content into already existing classes on campus. Additionally, the funding was used to identify methods of improving the quality of the campus climate for diversity.

In winter and spring 1992, the campus climate study was conceived and administered by the Office of Institutional Research at NSCC. More than 1,100 students from a variety of programs of study (vocational, basic skills, and academic transfer) were given written surveys to complete. The surveys contained demographic questions as well as opinion questions regarding the quality of the campus environment for students from diverse backgrounds. A separate but similar survey instrument was developed and administered to 450 NSCC employees (classified staff, full- and part-time faculty, and administrators).

Results from the climate study were summarized and presented for discussion by a focus group of multicultural student specialists during late summer of 1992. This focus group was videotaped, and a shortened version of the tape was presented to the campus community during fall Convocation Day. Afterwards, viewers were invited to participate in roundtable discussions of the themes that arose from the video and the surveys.

Among respondents to the student survey, a majority of students of all ethnic backgrounds spoke favorably of the campus climate for diversity at North Seattle Community College. Fewer, however, felt that the campus itself had enhanced their understanding of diversity. Students were asked to indicate their opinions regarding various strategies for improving cultural sensitivity on campus, and many suggested the inclusion of more information about ethnicity in their courses. Many also suggested that the college should work harder at attracting students of color to enroll on campus.

The climate study at NSCC increased the level of consciousness across campus about racial sensitivity. Its support by senior administrators signaled to members of the campus community that the college was serious about assessing and improving its racial climate. This study proved very effective in providing baseline data about campus attitudes before the start of new diversity programs. A follow-up climate study will be conducted in 1995–1996 in order to assess how much the climate has improved as a result of the various multicultural programs and courses implemented at the college.

In addition to the campus climate study, North Seattle Community College has conducted other assessment-related studies of multicultural student progress. In 1992—its second year of operation—the Office of Institutional Research at NSCC gathered baseline data on the enrollments, retention, and graduation rates of students of color in various areas of study. These data were summarized in a campus multicultural data fact book, which was presented to campus faculty, staff, and administrators early in 1993. Through this information, the campus was able to assess the educational progress and outcomes of students of color in vocational, academic transfer, and basic skills areas of study.

North Seattle Community College uses mission and goal statements as the institutional blueprint for outlining its long-term plans. Student learning outcome goals are developed on campus in a variety of areas—skills, knowledge, and attitudes. These outcomes are then used to define various degree and certificate general education requirements.

In addition to providing campuswide and systemwide data on performance of diverse students, the institutional research office at NSCC has served the campus mission and goals of serving diverse student needs by distributing information to interested faculty at departmental and course levels. Using this information, individual faculty members began to develop increased awareness of the differences in outcomes associated with students from various cultural and ethnic backgrounds.

In 1992, the college's social sciences division began a divisionwide assessment of courses to determine which new outcomes would be appropriate. An outcomes checklist was then developed and circulated to the faculty to match against specific courses—that is, assess whether the outcome was being taught in a specific course, and how much. A second checklist was developed to determine which of the selected outcomes were not offered. The division faculty then developed guidelines for two new faculty positions. Assessment of division resources (faculty and courses), reinforced by outcomes data, were used to convince senior administrators to hire two new faculty, one of whom specialized in multicultural issues.

The new multicultural instructor was hired to help other faculty redesign existing courses with an added multicultural curricular component, as well as to design new courses. Faculty training workshops on multicultural curriculum infusion were offered by the multicultural instructor using a combination of data and anecdotal means for discussing student outcomes. Campuswide workshops were also offered in cooperation with the office of institutional research in order to review and expand areas of multicultural campus research among faculty and staff. Additionally, a two-day retreat for all college faculty was offered by the multicultural instructor.

In providing resources for multicultural course development, the Title III grant enabled faculty to take release time so that they could make a number of changes. First, some faculty shifted existing course assignments. Examples included an English literature course in which all readings were by multicutural authors, an embedded ESL component in an allied health support class, and workshops teaching adapted ESL CATs to assess student outcomes. Second, new courses were the subject of pilot testing. An example involved ESL and psychology faculty developing and teaching a new ten-credit collaborative-learning course.

Summary

The needs of diverse students present a unique set of challenges on a college campus. We have discussed the need to develop awareness of the teaching and learning styles that most effectively benefit diverse students, but we have also cautioned against assumptions that the needs of such students are inherently different from those of traditional students. We have acknowledged that changes can be made both at the course or departmental level and at the institutional level that contribute to improved retention and graduation rates of diverse students. This is, arguably, one of the chief goals of any assessment effort—to increase the educational success of all students and to diminish differences in outcomes on the basis of race or ethnicity of enrolled students.

Perhaps the most important issue that must be confronted when assessment activities are conducted with the intent of improving the outcomes of diverse students is the policy issue: How can community colleges contribute to greater equity in American society among students from widely different backgrounds? Among the questions that policy makers, administrators, faculty, and staff must ask are these:

Should assessment programs be focused simply on measurement of differences or on changing outcomes in favor of addressing the special needs of the educationally underprepared?

Is there a campuswide commitment to improving outcomes of diverse students, or are there pockets of resistance within particular divisions of the college?

Is there a state policy on assessment that outlines specific, measurable goals and objectives for diverse students such as retention, transfer, and graduation rates?

How can educational professionals who are committed to improving the outcomes of diverse students continue to build connections both on and off their campuses with others who share their commitments and who want to share their ideas?

What resources (financial, personnel, informational) is the institution willing to devote to efforts at assessing and improving the outcomes of diverse students?

Many individuals on campus are already involved in assessment activities that directly or indirectly have an impact on diverse students. Offices of institutional research and outcomes assessment may be of great help in linking these individuals to others who wish to focus more on improving outcomes of these students. On campuses in which these offices are absent, instructional and student services administrators must take leadership positions in order to increase their institutions' commitment to improved successes of diverse students. It is only through broad-based efforts—across campus and across college boundaries—that assessment activities can truly begin to reduce the inequities of many diverse students' educational experiences.

SCOTT P. KERLIN is director of institutional planning and research, North Seattle Community College.

PATRICIA B. BRITZ is director of outcomes assessment, North Seattle Community College.

*Used with quantitative research, qualitative research results in a
more comprehensive and realistic appraisal of student outcomes
and institutional effectiveness.*

Qualitative Assessment: An Institutional Reality Check

Mary L. Mittler, Trudy H. Bers

Caught in the throes of what Stephen Spangehl in Chapter Two aptly calls
"datalust," many institutions focus virtually all their research resources and
attention on the collection, manipulation and application of data: raw numbers, percentages, percentiles, means, and scores on scales and standardized
tests. Then, often in splendid isolation, one or another administrator, faculty
member, or staff person interprets these data; the interpretation then is pro-
mulgated as truth.

Recognizing the need for data as well as the importance and worth of careful analysis and interpretation of them, we assert that assessment must include
qualitative research, a complementary way of collecting information about ourselves, our students, and our programs.

In this chapter, we will describe briefly three qualitative research projects
carried out at our college. We will demonstrate how these research projects
yielded considerable information about our students and our own internal
processes, and how that information sometimes complemented and sometimes
contradicted findings of quantitative research studies. The use of qualitative
research has often confirmed our perceptions, but occasionally has challenged
and forced us to revisit and refine them. Finally, we will indicate how the
results of such studies were used to improve the kinds and quality of our college programs and services.

Qualitative Research

Before beginning, we want to clarify what we mean by qualitative research. Following Fetterman (1991), we agree that qualitative research is characterized

by an interest in what people think and why they think what they think. Individuals' subjective perceptions of reality, regardless of whether these are consistent with "facts," are the topics of interest. Data are words, not numbers, and rarely is there an attempt to generalize to a larger population. Often the researcher is a member or participant in the group about whom he or she is attempting to learn; even where the researcher is not so involved, his or her role is to understand the context and nature of reality within which individuals operate *as they see it.*

There are many qualitative research techniques, including focus groups, in-depth interviewing, participant observation, and case studies. The projects we describe are not intended to illustrate any particular technique, but rather are presented to encourage readers to expand the range and type of work conducted at their institutions under the rubric of assessment, and to serve as a balance to the growing enthusiasm to report numbers as if they were proof of effectiveness.

We offer as support for our position two quite different but cogent reminders. The first is from Henry Mintzberg (1994), surely one of the most prolific and insightful students of organizational behavior, who in a recent *Harvard Business Review* article about strategic planning, much of which is directly relevant to the process of assessment, puts forth what he calls "soft analysis." The person who engages in soft analysis is intent on posing the right questions rather than finding the right answers. Qualitative research can help us to uncover the right questions, the questions raised by our students and ourselves about what we are doing and whether we are accomplishing our goals.

The second reminder is simpler yet. We are indebted to a speaker whose name we do not recall but whose wonderful statement we do: "You do not fatten a pig by weighing it." We cannot know all that we need to know about our students and institutions just by measuring and quantifying. Sometimes we need most to listen and to watch.

Assessment Audit

In early 1992, faculty members and others at the college were engaged in several projects focusing on student learning: the revision of our assessment and placement policies and procedures, the revision of our general education requirements, and the formulation of an institutional assessment plan. The impetus for these initiatives, to some extent, came from external sources: North Central Association criteria regarding outcomes assessment and institutional effectiveness; new state regulations and guidelines concerning a model general education component in associate degrees; and increased numbers of mandated state reports about accountability, productivity, priorities, quality, and efficiency. However, the major thrust behind each of these projects was our continuing need to ensure that students were being well-served by the college.

As work on these projects progressed, it became increasingly clear that although we knew that certain data had to be collected such as how many students were being served by various offices, who persisted in enrolling term after term, and how our students fared in placement tests, we often did not have any idea who collected these data, where they were stored, processed, and analyzed, and how they were used to make decisions. Finally, we decided that we needed to conduct an assessment audit in order to compile baseline information about what sorts of data and information about students were being gathered at the institution; how these data were stored, accessed, analyzed, and used; and the extent to which duplicative or potentially complementary assessments existed in isolation from each other.

We began by identifying every office on campus where student data of any kind might be collected, without attempting to prejudge whether such data were of value or whether such data were in fact being gathered. We wanted to know as much as possible about what kinds of data were available; we didn't want people to feel the need to justify their data collections—just to tell us about them. We agreed to personally contact and interview assigned people on our list. We used a common set of questions; recorded summaries of our conversations; and then jointly synthesized our findings.

Although this was a very time-consuming method, we believe we obtained far better results than would have been generated otherwise. People were pleased to be asked about their work; they were far more detailed in their responses than they might have been in writing. Some interviewees claimed initially that they did not collect any data about students and certainly did not engage in assessment, but further conversation elicited descriptions of activities that did involve data collection and assessment, but they had never been conceptualized as such. During the course of a conversation, it was not unusual to have someone allude to data kept in another office, data of which we were simply not aware. One interview would lead to another, and to another.

Our synthesis and the themes that emerged yielded important information. On one hand, we were able to confirm that we do collect a lot of information about our students. On the other, we do not share that information as well as we might. Consequently, several offices keep redundant data, wasting staff and student time and creating institutional inefficiencies. We also found that although data may be collected, they may also simply be stored—sometimes in cardboard boxes—and not put to use. Sometimes that was due to a lack of staff to manipulate and analyze the data; often people simply didn't know what could be done with the data at hand.

Because of findings such as these, we were able to discuss with various administrators, faculty, and staff ways to improve their data collections. In addition, the office of research began offering informational sessions to inform people within the institution about ways the office might assist them in gathering, managing, and analyzing data to address their own questions and concerns. Finally, we were able to inform the college committee charged with investigating the purchase of a new administrative computing system of some of the ways in which lack of a shared data base prevented the efficient and effective use of data.

Without the assessment audit, we might have been able to guess that some of what we found was true. With it, we were able to ground our suspicions in reality, provide some validation for people across the institution, who were delighted to see that someone cared about what they were doing, and make immediate changes—as well as recommend longer-term changes—to correct deficiencies that might have continued to go unnoticed.

Exit Interviews

Every year we engage in systematic research to give us information from former students about their perceptions of and their experiences at the college, but we know that these responses may be affected by the lapsed time between the administration of the survey and their enrollment here. Also, because alumni surveys are intended to assess a range of programs and services, they simply cannot provide a single area with in-depth information or insights about its services.

In 1991, our survey of alumni of baccalaureate programs revealed students' dissatisfaction with the advising process at the college. Clearly something was wrong, but the survey gave no indication of exactly what it was. The following spring, the vice president of student affairs initiated a series of individual exit interviews with a cadre of students drawn from graduates. Her goal was to try to delve deeper into students' perceptions of the advising process; at the same time, she wanted to probe for other information relevant to questions of student development. She was interested in knowing whether students' goals changed while attending the college; what students learned about the decision making process, about taking responsibility for themselves, about getting along with people different from themselves, and about working their way through a bureaucracy; how students learned where to go for help. She also wanted students to know that the college was interested in knowing how effectively they had been served and that their opinions mattered. Because she wanted as many people in her area as possible involved in the project, student affairs administrators, faculty, and staff were asked to serve as interviewers.

One hundred fifty students were targeted and sent a letter asking if they would be willing to be interviewed. A follow-up phone call was made to approximately half of those to whom letters were sent and appointments made with the twenty-six students who agreed to participate. Each interview followed the same protocol; the results were summarized and used as the basis for several discussions within the area of student affairs and, as warranted by information gathered, with others as well.

The following spring, the project was repeated. However, this time the decision was made to expand the pool of students to those who had completed between fifty and sixty hours of credit at the college. Because many of our students choose not to graduate, but to transfer or stop out before that time, having graduation status as the sole criterion for eligibility seemed too limiting. The methodology remained the same.

Again, this research project was very time-consuming, but the information gathered was valuable and simply would not have been available to the institution by other means. Students who participated were pleased to have the opportunity to talk with a live person about their college careers; they were willing to expand on their ideas much more readily and expansively than if they had been asked to do so in writing. For nonnative speakers of English especially, a conversation seemed a more comfortable venue of expression.

Did this process provide more information about how students experienced the advising process? Indeed, and when their experiences were not positive ones, the interview process allowed us to determine exactly why that was. One of the most common complaints was that students felt they needed advice about their academic choices much earlier in their career at the college. Many students felt that waiting to seek academic advice until they were ready to graduate or transfer was to their disadvantage. Although we could argue that students themselves must take responsibility for seeking out such information, such would not solve the problem. Instead, student affairs implemented an "advising hold," requiring students to see a counselor or sign a waiver form before registering for their thirtieth credit hour.

One other significant finding of the study was the response students gave to the question "Where do you go to find help?" Colleges (and we are no exception here) spend inordinate sums of money printing catalogs, course guides, pamphlets, and brochures in the hope of telling students all they need to know to succeed and where to go to have almost any question answered or problem addressed. Our students told us that it was not from printed material that they found guidance; students found help from teachers, friends, counselors, and librarians—from people. In the 1993 study, only a handful of forty-two interviewed said that they found help in the printed material. As a result of this information, renewed emphasis was put on communicating directly and personally with students, and strategies were developed that incorporated this goal. Volunteers roamed the registration lines offering help to students struggling to decipher class schedules and application forms; the pool of faculty advisors available to work with students was expanded; people were stationed at the main entrances to the college on the first days of class to give directions and answer questions.

The study also confirmed for those who work in student affairs that students greatly value learning that relates closely to self-development. Often, more formal and quantitative research addresses academic issues and concerns. There is no denying that institutions need to know whether students found their classes challenging, whether they were prepared for higher-level course work or for employment, and whether their courses transferred, but it is also important for us to know whether students were helped to develop in other ways. The interview project allowed us to use a personal approach to explore with students issues of personal growth and to validate by yet another means the importance of some vital, albeit less visible, student services.

Focus Groups

The assessment audit and exit interview share a common approach: both used individual conversations between an interviewer and interviewee to gather information. In both instances, interviewers followed a general set of questions, but the primary thrust was to carry on a nonthreatening conversation with a single person about a particular topic.

Focus groups share most of these same attributes, except that by definition they are conversations among several people—usually eight to ten—who are guided in their discussion by a moderator. The literature about how to do focus groups continues to grow, although uncovering examples of actual focus group projects in community colleges is more challenging because few of these projects are published, indexed, or even available in written form (Bers, 1994).

The focus group project we describe here is one we held with high school students. Anxious to learn what they thought of some college publications, especially a semiannual newsletter ostensibly targeted to them and their parents, we sought the assistance of an external market research supplier to recruit participants who met our selection criteria: high school juniors and seniors who were in the middle third of their classes and attended schools in our district. The group was held at the supplier's office to take advantage of their focus group room, to provide space for observers from the college, to allow audio taping, and to distance participants from the fact that our institution was conducting the project.

We learned from the participants about the attributes and characteristics of publications to which they responded, about what they didn't like or wish to read, and about their overall perceptions of the college. We learned that a recruitment brochure created some years ago, which was highly controversial within the institution, met with strong but mixed reaction among young teens. We learned that it might be better not to produce certain publications at all if they did not meet threshold expectations about quality and that our zeal to give potential students information we thought important exceeded their attention span. By having college staff members observe the group, we were able to watch how participants handled materials, to see their expressions and listen to the tone of their voices. All these provide important clues about how they view reality.

As a result of our focus groups, we decided to discontinue the newsletter targeted to high school students and to consider, instead, incorporating some of the articles intended for this audience into the college's more comprehensive newsletter sent to all households and businesses in the community. We have also begun to rethink the types of photographs used in our publications and to contain our propensity to overwhelm readers with more detail than they wish to read.

Some Final Observations About Qualitative Research

Findings from qualitative research are valuable because they reveal how individuals perceive their world in their own words, with their own values, not because of numbers, percents, or measures—"how many" or "how much." By putting college personnel together with the individuals whose worlds they seek to understand—with faculty and staff for the assessment audit and with students for the other two projects—the qualitative research studies described in this article enriched understanding, led to improved programs and services, and served as forceful reminders that no matter how intense is the pressure on colleges to become more businesslike in our analyses and work processes, education is at base a labor-intensive, people-oriented venture.

Quantitative research—numbers—tell us something, but not everything. Qualitative research tells us other things. Institutions that recognize the contribution both approaches make to assessment and understanding will be well-served and will serve their constituencies better than those engaging only in number counting or storytelling.

References

Bers, T. H. "Focus Group Research: Community College Applications." *Journal of Applied Research in Community College,* in press.

Fetterman, D. M. (ed.). *Using Qualitative Methods in Institutional Research.* New Directions for Institutional Research, no. 72. San Francisco: Jossey-Bass, 1991.

Mintzberg, H. "The Fall and Rise of Strategic Planning." *Harvard Business Review,* Jan.–Feb. 1994, pp. 107–114.

MARY L. MITTLER is assistant vice president for educational services and dean at Oakton Community College, Des Plaines, Illinois.

TRUDY H. BERS is senior director of research, curriculum, and planning at Oakton Community College, Des Plaines, Illinois.

Thirteen methodological options for assessing student learning and development are presented, and the advantages, disadvantages, ways to reduce the disadvantages, and bottom-line strategies provide guidelines for selecting suitable methods.

A Critical Review of Student Assessment Options

Joseph Prus, Reid Johnson

Whether the goal is to assess an objective in basic skills, general education, the major, career preparation, or student personal growth and development, one overriding truism applies: good methodological choices produce results useful for program enhancement and poor methodological choices are detrimental to that process.

Complicating the method selection process—especially for those inexperienced in probability theory, program evaluation, and principles of psychoeducational measurement—are some additional facts of higher education assessment (HEA):

There will always be more than one way to measure any objective; there are always options.

No single method is good for measuring a wide variety of different student abilities; there is no one true way.

We cannot rely on popularity, tradition, sales propaganda, or primary and secondary education practices to separate the assessment wheat from the chaff in higher education; it isn't simply a matter of choosing the most attractive available option.

As in virtually all other domains of human assessment, there is a consistently inverse correlation between the quality of measurement methods and their

This work was partially supported by grants from the Fund for the Improvement of Post Secondary Education, the South Carolina Commission on Higher Education, and Winthrop University.

expediency; the best methods usually take longer and cost more faculty time, student effort, and money.
The only way to be certain that a particular methodological option is good for your program is to pilot-test it on your students, in your curriculum, with your faculty—an educated trial-and-error approach.

What we are recommending in terms of method selection, therefore, is a two-step process. First, use the literature, conferences, models, and methods from other institutions, as well as consultations to tentatively identify a range of methods that appear to fit your needs and standards of quality. Second, pilot-test the best candidates on a limited trial basis with a representative student sample at your institution. Proceed to full-scale implementation only with methods that are valid for your programs.

Validity—the key selection criterion for any HEA option—is made up of three equally vital attributes: relevance (the option measures your educational objective as directly as possible); accuracy (the option measures your educational objective as precisely as possible); and utility (the option provides formative and summative results with clear implications for educational program evaluation and improvement). If an assessment method doesn't measure what your program teaches, or doesn't measure it with precision, or doesn't suggest what the program's strengths and weaknesses are, then that assessment method cannot serve the institutional effectiveness goals of your program.

Although finding an ideal assessment method for each educational objective is probably unrealistic, we should strive for that goal in order to maximize the effectiveness and efficiency of our assessment efforts. Some characteristics of an ideal method include maximum relevance to the unique aspects of the local program curriculum (internal validity); maximum generalizability to similar programs at colleges across the state, region, and nation (external validity); results useful for evaluating both program objectives and individual student progress; maximum incorporation into activities in the ongoing academic program; minimum latency between assessment and educationally useful results; and a reasonable outlay of time, effort, and money.

It is also important to recognize that the validity of any student assessment method can be effectively evaluated only in relation to the educational objective to be measured. A method may be very relevant, accurate, and useful for assessing some objectives but invalid for assessing others. Thus, a review of methodological assessment options must take into account the types of educational objectives for which each option might be suited. Objectives for student learning and development can be classified as student knowledge, or the quantity and quality of information acquired toward an educational objective; skills, or the abilities acquired toward an educational objective; attitudes, or the feelings, values, motives, and other affective orientations toward an educational objective; behavior, or the actions or habitual patterns that express an educational objective; or some combination of these learning and development indicators.

Taking these and other educationally, statistically, and practically important factors into account, the most common methodological options for assessing student learning and development in higher education are briefly reviewed in the following section. The relative advantages and disadvantages of various types of tests, competency-based methods, self-reports and third-party reports, and other methods are outlined. Possible means by which to reduce the disadvantages associated with each method are also provided.

Assessment Methods

I. Tests (demand–response tasks using standard stimulus items and pre-established criteria for "correctness or incorrectness" scoring).
  A. Commercial, Norm-Referenced, Standardized Exams (group-administered, mostly or entirely multiple-choice, "objective" tests in one or more curricular areas; scores are based on comparison with a reference or norm group).
  Advantages
  - Can be adopted and implemented quickly.
  - Reduce or eliminate faculty time demands in instrument development and grading (relatively low front-loading and back-loading effort).
  - Are scored objectively.
  - Provide for externality of measurement (external validity).
  - Provide reference group comparison often required by mandates.
  - May be beneficial or required in instances where state or national standards exist for the discipline or profession.
  Disadvantages
  - Limit what can be measured to relatively superficial knowledge or learning.
  - Eliminate the important process of learning and clarification of goals and objectives typically associated with local development of measurement instruments.
  - Unlikely to measure the specific goals and objectives of a program, department, or institution.
  - Relative standing tends to be less meaningful than criterion-referenced results for program and student evaluation purposes.
  - Norm-referenced data are dependent on the institutions in comparison groups and methods of selecting students to be tested in those institutions. (Caution: unlike many norm-referenced tests, such as those measuring intelligence, present norm-referenced tests in higher education generally do not use randomly selected or well-stratified national samples.)
  - Group-administered multiple-choice tests always include a potentially high degree of error, usually not correctable by "guessing correction" formulae (lower validity).

- Provide summative data only (no formative evaluation).
- Results are unlikely to have direct implications for program improvement or individual student progress.
- Results are highly susceptible to misinterpretation and misuse both within and outside the institution.

Ways to Reduce Disadvantages

- Choose test carefully, and only after faculty have reviewed available instruments and determined a satisfactory degree of match between the test and the curriculum.
- Request and review technical data, especially reliability and validity data and information on normative sample from test publishers.
- Use on-campus measurement experts to review reports of test results and create more customized summary reports for the institution and faculty.
- Whenever possible, choose tests that also provide criterion-referenced results.
- Ensure that such tests are only one aspect of a multimethod approach in which no firm conclusions based on norm-referenced data are reached without cross-validation from other sources.

Bottom Line

They are relatively quick, easy, and inexpensive, but useful mostly where group-level performance and external comparisons of results are required. Not as useful for individual student or program evaluation.

B. Locally Developed Exams (objective or subjective tests designed by faculty of the program being evaluated).

Advantages

- Content and style can be geared to specific goals, objectives, and student characteristics of the institution, program, or curriculum.
- Specific criteria for performance can be established in relationship to curriculum.
- Process of development can lead to clarification or crystallization of what is important in the process and content of student learning.
- Local grading by faculty can provide immediate feedback related to material considered meaningful.
- Provide greater faculty and institutional control over interpretation and use of results.
- Provide more direct implication of results for program improvements.

Disadvantages

- Require considerable leadership and coordination, especially during the various phases of development.
- Are costly in terms of time and effort (more initial effort for objective; more follow-up effort for subjective).
- Demand expertise in measurement to ensure validity, reliability, and utility.

- May not provide for externality (degree of objectivity associated with review and comparisons external to the program or institution).

Ways to Reduce Disadvantages

- Enter into consortium with other programs, departments, or institutions with similar goals as a means of reducing costs associated with developing instruments. An element of externality is also added through this approach, especially if used for test grading as well as development.
- Use on-campus measurement experts whenever possible for test construction and validation.
- Contract with faculty consultants to provide development and grading.
- Incorporate outside experts and community leaders into the development and grading process.
- Include requirements for maximum relevance with minimum disruption (a "capstone" course).
- Validate results through consensus with other data.

Bottom Line

Most useful for individual student or program evaluation, with careful adherence to measurement principles. Must be supplemented for external validity.

C. Oral Examination (an evaluation of student knowledge levels through a face-to-face interrogative dialogue with program faculty). Oral exams generally have the same basic strengths and weaknesses of local tests plus the following advantages and disadvantages:

Advantages

- Allows measurement of student achievement in considerably greater depth and breadth through follow-up questions, probes, and encouragement of detailed clarifications (increased internal validity and formative evaluation of student abilities).
- Nonverbal (paralinguistic and visual) cues aid interpretation of student responses.
- Dialogue format decreases miscommunications and misunderstandings in both questions and answers.
- Rapport-gaining techniques can reduce test anxiety, help focus and maintain maximum student attention and effort.
- Dramatically increases formative evaluation of student learning (clues as to how and why they reached their answers).
- Identifies and decreases error variance due to guessing.
- Provides process evaluation of student thinking and speaking skills along with knowledge content.

Disadvantages

- Requires considerably more faculty time because oral exams must be conducted one-to-one or with very small groups of students.
- Can inhibit student responsiveness due to intimidation, face-to-face pressures, or lack of oral facility. (May have similar effects on some faculty!)

- Inconsistencies of administration and probing across students reduces standardization and generalizability of results (potentially lower external validity).

Ways to Reduce Disadvantages

- Prearrange standard questions, most common follow-up probes, and how to deal with typical students' problem responses; use training simulations.
- Take time to establish open, nonthreatening atmosphere for testing.
- Electronically record oral exams for more detailed evaluation later.

Bottom Line

Oral exams can provide excellent results, but usually only with significant—perhaps prohibitive—additional cost. Definitely worth using in programs with fewer students and for the highest priority objectives in any program.

II. Competency-Based Methods (measuring preoperationalized abilities in most direct, real-world approach).

A. Performance Appraisals (systematic measurement of overt demonstration of acquired skills).

Advantages

- Provide a more direct measure of what has been learned (presumably in the program).
- Go beyond paper-and-pencil tests and most other assessment methods in measuring skills.
- Are preferable to most other methods in measuring the application and generalization of learning to specific settings and situations.
- Are particularly relevant to the goals and objectives of professional training programs and disciplines with well-defined skill development.

Disadvantages

- Ratings and grading are typically more subjective than for standardized tests.
- Require considerable time and effort (especially front-loading), and are thus costly.
- Sample of behavior observed or performance appraised may not be typical, especially because of the presence of observers.

Ways to Reduce Disadvantages

- Develop specific, operational (measurable) criteria for observing and appraising performance.
- Provide training for observers and appraisers.
- Conduct pilot-testing in which rate of agreement (inter-rater reliability) between observers or appraisers is determined. Continue training or alter criteria until acceptable consistency of measurement is obtained.
- Conduct observations or appraisals in the least obtrusive manner possible (use one-way observational mirrors or video cameras).
- Observe and appraise behavior in multiple situations and settings.

- Consider training and using graduate students, upper-level students, and community volunteers as a means of reducing the cost and time demands on faculty.
- Cross-validate results with other measures.

Bottom Line

Generally the most highly valued but costly form of student outcomes assessment—usually the most valid way to measure skill development.

B. Simulation (primarily used to approximate the results of performance appraisal, when direct demonstration of the student skill is impractical due to the target competency involved, logistical problems, or cost).

Advantages

- Better means of evaluating depth and breadth of student skill development than tests or other nonperformance-based measures.
- Very flexible; some degree of simulation can be arranged for virtually any student target skill.
- For many skills, can be group-administered, thus providing an excellent combination of quality and economy.

Disadvantages

- For difficult skills, the higher the quality of simulation, the greater the likelihood of the problems of performance appraisal (such as cost and subjectivity; see "Performance Appraisals").
- Usually requires considerable planning and preparation.
- More expensive than traditional testing options in the short run.

Ways to Reduce Disadvantages

- Reducing problems is relatively easy because degree of simulation can be matched for maximum validity practicable for each situation.
- Can often be standardized through use of computer programs.

Bottom Line

An excellent means of increasing the external and internal validity of skills assessment at minimal long-term costs.

III. Self-Reports and Third-Party Reports (asking individuals to share their perceptions of their own attitudes and behaviors or those of others).

A. Written Surveys and Questionnaires (including direct or mailed, signed or anonymous).

Advantages

- Typically yield the perspective that students, alumni, and the public have of the institution, which may lead to changes especially beneficial to relationships with these groups.
- Convey a sense of importance regarding the opinions of constituent groups.
- Can cover a broad range of content areas in a brief period of time.
- Results tend to be more easily understood by lay persons.
- Can cover areas of learning and development that might be difficult or costly to assess more directly.

- Can provide accessibility to people who otherwise would be difficult to include in assessment efforts (alumni, parents, employers).

Disadvantages

- Results tend to be highly dependent on wording of items, salience of survey or questionnaire, and organization of instrument. Good surveys and questionnaires are more difficult to construct than they seem.
- Often rely on volunteer samples, which tend to be biased.
- Mail surveys tend to yield low response rates.
- Require careful organization in order to facilitate data analysis via computer for large samples.
- Commercially prepared surveys tend not to be entirely relevant to an individual institution and its students.
- Forced-response choices may not allow respondents to express their true opinions.
- Results reflect perceptions individuals are willing to report and thus tend to consist of indirect data.
- Locally developed instrument may not provide external references for results.

Ways to Reduce Disadvantages

- Use only carefully constructed instruments that have been reviewed by survey experts.
- Include open-ended, respondent-worded items along with forced-choice.
- If random sampling or surveying of the entire target population is not possible, obtain the maximum sample size possible and follow up with nonrespondents (preferably in person or by phone).
- If commercially prepared surveys are used, add locally developed items relevant to the institution.
- If locally developed surveys are used, attempt to include at least some external-reference items (from surveys for which national data are available).
- Word reports cautiously to reflect the fact that results represent perceptions and opinions respondents are willing to share publicly.
- Use pilot or try out samples in local development of instruments and request formative feedback from respondents on content clarity, sensitivity, and format.
- Cross-validate results through other sources of data.

Bottom Line

A relatively inexpensive way to collect data on important evaluative topics from a large number of respondents. Must always be treated cautiously, however, because results reflect only what subjects are willing to report about their perception of their attitudes and behaviors.

B. Exit Interview and Other Interviews (evaluating student reports of their attitudes and behaviors in a face-to-face interrogative dialogue).

Advantages
- Student interviews tend to have most of the attributes of surveys and questionnaires with the exception of requiring direct contact, which may limit accessibility to certain populations.
- Allow for more individualized questions and follow-up probes based on the responses of interviewees.
- Provide immediate feedback.
- Include same observational and formative advantages as oral examinations.
- Often yield benefits beyond data collection that come from opportunities to interact with students and other groups.
- Can include a greater variety of items than is possible on surveys and questionnaires, including those that provide more direct measures of learning and development.

Disadvantages
- Require direct contact, which may be difficult to arrange.
- May be intimidating to interviewees, thus biasing results in the positive direction.
- Results tend to be highly dependent on wording of items and the manner in which interviews are conducted.
- Time-consuming, especially if large numbers of people are to be interviewed.

Ways to Reduce Disadvantages
- Plan the interviews carefully with assistance from experts.
- Provide training sessions for interviewers that include guidance in putting interviewees at ease and related interview skills.
- Interview random samples of students when it is not feasible to interview all.
- Conduct telephone interviews when face-to-face contact is not feasible.
- Develop an interview format and questions with a set time limit in mind.
- Conduct pilot-testing of interview and request interviewee formative feedback.
- Interview small groups when individual interviewing is not possible or is too costly.

Bottom Line
Interviews provide opportunities to cover a broad range of content and to interact with respondents. Opportunities to follow up on responses can be very valuable. Direct contact may be difficult to arrange, costly, and potentially threatening to respondents unless carefully planned.

C. Third-Party Reports (influences regarding student and alumni attitudes or observations on student and alumni behaviors made by someone other than the student or assessor, such as parents, faculty, or employers).

Advantages

Third-party reports have attributes similar to student self-reports, plus the following additional advantages:

- Can provide unique consumer input, valuable in its own right (especially employers and parents). How is our college serving their purposes?
- Offer different perspectives, presumably less biased than either student or assessor.
- Enable recognition and contact with important, often undervalued constituents. May improve relations simply by asking for their input.
- Can increase both internal validity (through convergent validity or triangulation with other data) and external validity (by adding more natural perspective).

Disadvantages

Third-party reports have disadvantages similar to those of self-reports, plus the following:

- As with any indirect data, inference and reports risk high degree of error.
- Third parties can be less biased, in directions more difficult to anticipate than self-reports.
- Less investment by third parties in assessment processes often means response rates even lower than those of students or alumni.
- Usually involves more logistical problems (identifying sample, making contact, and getting useful responses) and may cost more than expected.
- If information about individuals is requested, confidentiality becomes an important and sometimes problematic issue that must be addressed carefully.

Ways to Reduce Disadvantages

- Conduct face-to-face or phone interviews wherever possible, increasing validity through probing and formative evaluation during dialogue.
- Very careful, explicit directions for types and perspectives of responses requested can reduce variability.
- Attain informed consent in cases where information about individuals is being requested.
- Coordinate contacts with other campus organizations contacting the same groups to reduce "harassment" syndrome and increase response rates.
- Other self-report and interview ways to reduce disadvantages apply here as well.

Bottom Line

Third-party reports are valuable in that they access important data sources usually missed by other methods, but they can be problematic in cost of implementation and in gaining access to respondents. If personally identifiable information about individual students or alumni is requested, informed consent is needed.

IV. Other Measures
  A. Behavioral Observations (measuring the frequency, duration, and topology of student actions, usually in a natural setting with noninteractive methods).
    Advantages
    • Best way to evaluate degree to which attitudes and values are put into action.
    • Catching students being themselves is the most natural form of assessment.
    • Least intrusive assessment option; purpose is to avoid any interference with typical student activities.
    Disadvantages
    • Always some risk of confounded results due to observer effect; subjects may behave atypically if they know they are being observed.
    • Depending on the target behavior, there may be socially or professionally sensitive issues to be dealt with (invasion of privacy on student political activities or living arrangements) or even legal considerations (substance abuse or campus crime).
    • May encourage "Big Brother" perception of assessment or institution.
    • Inexperienced or inefficient observers can produce unreliable, invalid results.
    Ways to Reduce Disadvantages
    • Avoid socially or ethically sensitive target behaviors, especially initially.
    • Include representative student input in process of determining sensitivity of potential target behaviors.
    • Use electronic observers (audio and video recorders) wherever possible for accurate, reliable, permanent observation record (although this may increase cost in the short run if equipment is not already available).
    • Strictly adhere to ethical guidelines for the protection of research subjects.
    Bottom Line
    This is the best way to know what students actually do, how they manifest their motives, attitudes, and values. Special care and planning are required for sensitive target behaviors, but it is usually worth it for highly valid, useful results.
  B. External Examiner (using an expert in the field from outside your program—usually from a similar program at another institution—to conduct, evaluate, or supplement the assessment of your students).
    Advantages
    • Increases impartiality, third-party objectivity (external validity).
    • Feedback useful for both student and program evaluation. With a knowledgeable and cooperative (or well-paid) examiner, provides an opportunity for a valuable program consultation.

- May stimulate other collaborative efforts between departments or institutions.

Disadvantages

- Always some risk of a misfit between examiner's expertise or expectations and program outcomes.
- For individualized evaluations or large programs, can be very costly and time-consuming.

Ways to Reduce Disadvantages

- Share program philosophy and objectives and agree on assessment criteria beforehand.
- Form reciprocal external examiner consortia among similar programs to minimize costs, swapping external evaluations back and forth.
- Limit external examiner process to program areas where externality may be most helpful.

Bottom Line

Best used as a supplement to other assessment methods to enhance external validity, but not as the primary method. Other benefits can be accrued from the cross-fertilization that often results from using external examiners.

C. Archival Records (biographical, academic, or other file data available from college or other agencies and institutions).

Advantages

- Tend to be readily available, thus requiring little additional effort.
- Make further use of efforts that have already occurred.
- Cost-efficient.
- Constitute unobtrusive measurement, not requiring additional time or effort from students or other groups.
- Very useful for longitudinal studies.

Disadvantages

- Especially in large institutions, may require considerable effort and coordination to determine exactly what data are available campuswide.
- If individual records are included, may raise concerns regarding protection of rights and confidentiality.
- Easy availability may discourage the development of other measures of learning and development.
- May encourage attempts to find ways to use data rather than measurement related to specific goals and objectives.

Ways to Reduce Disadvantages

- Early in the development of an assessment program, conduct a comprehensive review of existing assessment and evaluation efforts and data being collected throughout the institution and its units ("campus data map").

- Be familiar with the Family Educational Rights and Privacy Act (Buckley Amendment) and avoid personally identifiable data collection without permission. Ensure security and protection of records.
- Use only archival records that are relevant to specific goals and objectives of learning and development.

Bottom Line

Relatively quick, easy, and cost-effective method. Usually limited data quality but integral to valuable longitudinal comparisons. Should be a standard component of all assessment programs.

D. Portfolios (collections of multiple student work samples, usually compiled over time).

Advantages

- Can be used to view learning and development longitudinally (for example, samples of student writing over time), which is a most valid and useful perspective.
- Multiple components of a curriculum can be measured (such as writing, critical thinking, and research skills) at the same time.
- Samples in a portfolio are more likely than test results to reflect student ability when planning, input from others, and similar opportunities common to most work settings are available (which increases generalizability or external validity of results).
- The process of reviewing and grading portfolios provides an excellent opportunity for faculty exchange and development, discussion of curriculum goals and objectives, review of grading criteria, and program feedback.
- Economical in terms of student time and effort because no separate assessment administration time is required.
- Greater faculty control over interpretation and use of results.
- Results are more likely to be meaningful at all levels (the individual student, program, or institution) and can be used for diagnostic and prescriptive purposes as well.
- Avoids or minimizes test anxiety and other one-shot measurement problems.
- Increases power of maximum performance measures over more artificial or restrictive speed measures on test or in-class sample.
- Increases student participation (selection, revision, and evaluation) in the assessment process.

Disadvantages

- Costly in terms of evaluator time and effort.
- Management of the collection and grading process, including the establishment of reliable and valid grading criteria, is likely to be challenging.
- May not provide for externality.

- If samples to be included have been previously submitted for course grades, faculty may be concerned that a hidden agenda of the process is to validate their grading.
- Security concerns may arise as to whether submitted samples are the students' own work or adhere to other measurement criteria.

Ways to Reduce Disadvantages

- Consider having portfolios submitted as part of a course requirement, especially a "capstone" course at the end of a program.
- Use portfolios from representative samples of students rather than having all students participate (this approach may save considerable time, effort, and expense but be problematic in other ways).
- Have more than one rater for each portfolio; establish inter-rater reliability through piloting designed to fine-tune rating criteria.
- Provide training for raters.
- Recognize that portfolios in which samples are selected by the students probably represent their best work.
- Cross-validate portfolios with more controlled student work samples (in-class tests and reports) for increased validity and security.

Bottom Line

Portfolios are a potentially valuable option adding important longitudinal and qualitative data in a more natural way. Particular care must be taken to maintain validity. Especially good for multiple-objective assessment.

E. Classroom Research (the use of a variety of relatively simple, quick, and easy-to-analyze assessment techniques that provide teachers with feedback on student responses to instruction, including achievement, interest, skills, and development).

Advantages

- Provides direct feedback to teachers with minimum latency, enabling fine-tuning of instruction.
- Encourages teachers to make goals and objectives explicit and to use assessment techniques that address such goals and objectives.
- Is a multimethod approach to assessment in itself.
- Is directly linked to teaching and learning.
- Is a good process measure.
- Tends to convey a genuine interest in students' learning.
- Tends to be a powerful vehicle for faculty development.

Disadvantages

- The relative simplicity of techniques may encourage their misuse by faculty who lack understanding of the foundations and principles of classroom research.
- Results typically based on small sample sizes.
- Difficult to replicate and generalize results.
- Standardization and validation of instruments and techniques are problematic for institutional assessment purposes.

- Not as useful for curriculum design and policy making due to lack of "product" emphasis.

Ways to Reduce Disadvantages
- Provide training and support for faculty.
- Establish faculty teams to assess student skills of mutual interest.
- Encourage the development, adoption, and pilot testing of techniques that might be used across classes to assess student learning related to a common goal in the major or general education program.
- Ensure that results are not used punitively against individual faculty researchers.

Bottom Line
Classroom research methods are very good for quick, specific feedback for instructional improvement at the course level, but less useful for overall program evaluation purposes.

Summary

The most valid methods (for each student objective) produce the most useful results. Invalid methods yield useless or misleading results, which may leave you worse off than when you started. All assessment options have advantages and disadvantages. An effective comprehensive assessment program seeks to maximize strengths of methods while minimizing disadvantages.

It is crucial to use a multimethod and multisource approach to assessment in order to obtain maximum validity and to reduce potential error or bias associated with any one approach. Always consider initial implementation of an assessment method as a pilot test, then seek to validate the method and results through comparisons with results from other methods or sources. In other words, be cautious in using any one method and in interpreting results.

Search for ideal methods, but recognize that the ideal usually means methods that are the best fit between program needs, satisfactory validity, and affordability. Recognize that development of an assessment program is a dynamic process. Ongoing assessment of assessment methods themselves is an important part of that process.

JOSEPH PRUS is professor of psychology and director of the office of assessment at Winthrop University, Rock Hill, South Carolina.

REID JOHNSON is professor of psychology, Winthrop University, and director of the South Carolina Higher Education Assessment Network.

This annotated bibliography on institutional assessment in two-year colleges includes publications on assessment methods, student outcomes studies, the use of assessment as a planning tool, and general articles.

Sources and Information: Assessment and the Community College

Elizabeth Foote

What constitutes an effective community college? To measure their accomplishments, two-year schools collect a wide variety of data ranging from student success rates to achievement of mission statement goals. With greater accountability demanded of community colleges by states and accrediting agencies, evaluation of effectiveness continues to be important.

The following publications reflect the current ERIC literature on institutional assessment in community colleges. Most ERIC documents (publications with ED numbers) can be viewed on microfiche at approximately nine hundred libraries worldwide. In addition, most may be ordered on microfiche or on paper from the ERIC Document Reproduction Service (EDRS) at (800) 443-ERIC.

General Articles

These articles provide an overview of institutional assessment.

Afshar, A. "The Attributive Theory of Quality: A Model for Quality Measurement in Higher Education." Ph.D. dissertation, University of Florida, 1991. 81 pp. (ED 336 403)

A theoretical basis for defining and measuring the quality of institutions of higher education, namely for accreditation purposes, is developed. The theory, the attributive theory of quality, is illustrated using a calculation model based on general systems theory. The theory postulates that quality exists only in relation to the phenomenon to which it is attributed. Quality can be defined by its attributes and can be quantified by developing a system of numeric values for the attributes. An intersubjective approach to data collection and analysis requiring participation by experts is recommended.

Aumack, B., and Blake, L. J. *Texas State Technical College Review.* Austin: Texas Higher Education Coordinating Board, 1992. 14 pp. (ED 355 993)

To begin the review process, a review team was recruited by the Texas Higher Education Coordinating Board and, in keeping with the legislative requirements, findings were sought with regard to campus locations, student enrollment trends, funding mechanisms, physical facilities, industry support, and the need for technically trained workers in Texas. Principal findings and recommendations, based on site tours, interviews, and analysis of existing reports, include the following: (1) the system's four campuses were found to be fulfilling their legislative mandate, and the five extension centers were found to be more like community colleges than technical colleges, serving local needs and populations; (2) current funding for the Texas State Technical College System (TSTCS) is inadequate and special funding formulas should be developed to meet the TSTCS's operating and capital costs; (3) the TSTCS should limit its programmatic growth to advanced and emerging technologies, phasing out other programs; (4) the TSTCS should be limited to three regional campuses (at Waco, Harlingen, and Sweetwater), with current additional facilities becoming independent community colleges or part of the state community college system; and (5) the TSTCS should recruit students on a statewide basis.

Cannon, D. T., and others. *Institutional Effectiveness Resource Manual.* Columbia: South Carolina State Board for Technical and Comprehensive Education, 1992. 400 pp. (ED 358 874)

This resource manual was produced to assist the South Carolina Technical College System's efforts to improve institutional effectiveness and accountability. The first two sections of the manual provide a brief foreword, a description of state initiatives for research and academic excellence in South Carolina, the text of state legislation requiring annual reports from public postsecondary institutions on institutional effectiveness, and memoranda providing clarifying information about the reports. The next section presents information on the Southern Association of Colleges and Schools' accreditation requirements for planning, evaluation, and institutional research. The next section presents the 1990–1991 Commission on Higher Education reports for technical colleges, providing information on student persistence, alumni follow-up study results, student retention, and racial equality in student and faculty demographics. The final sections provide sample methodologies and surveys, a bibliography of selected articles on assessment and educational measurement and information on selected educational outcomes measures, definitions, a bibliography of assessment instruments and articles, and the minutes of the coordinators' meetings.

Gibson, K. "A Report to the Kansas Council of Instructional Administrators on Institutional Effectiveness Assessment and Student Academic Achievement." Overland Park, Kans.: Johnson County Community College. 1992. 16 pp. (ED 352 077)

In July and August 1992, a subcommittee of the Kansas Council of Instructional Administrators sent a questionnaire to the deans of instruction at Kansas's community colleges to obtain information on each college's institutional effectiveness assessment plans. Survey findings, based on a 100 percent response rate from the nineteen deans, included the following: (1) 79 percent of the deans indicated that the colleges had engaged in a review of their mission statements as a preparation for assessing institutional effectiveness, but only 47 percent had involved students in the review process; (2) only six deans viewed faculty members as strongly committed to the process of institutional effectiveness assessment; (3) only 42 percent of the colleges had developed a formal plan or model for assessing institutional effectiveness; (4) although most colleges conducted formal evaluations of academic programs, few used student outcomes–based evaluation; (5) the most frequently used measures of student achievement were retention rate, grade distribution analysis, pass rates on licensure exams, and employment rates; (6) at twelve colleges, the evaluation of faculty was considered part of the institutional assessment process; and (7) 74 percent of the deans reported that sustaining long-term faculty support represented a significant obstacle to the successful implementation of an institutional assessment plan.

Hudgins, J. L. "Institutional Effectiveness: A Maturing Movement. Where Do We Go from Here?" Paper presented at the Fifth Summer Institute of the Community College Consortium, Madison, Wis., June 21, 1993. 61 pp. (ED 358 891)

In the eighth year of the assessment movement, more than forty states have educational mandates for measuring institutional effectiveness; all six accrediting regions have incorporated assessment of student learning as a condition for accreditation; and in a 1991 survey, 90 percent of responding colleges reported that they are doing something in the area of assessment. Although some exemplary assessment practices can be identified, the majority of institutions are making minimal efforts. There are three major difficulties in implementing accountability efforts at the state level: the inability of institutions to produce evidence of effective performance, uneven institutional responses, and poor communication.

Assessment Methods

Community colleges have developed several methods to quantify their effectiveness.

Blanzy, J. J., and Sucher, J. E. "Technology: The Silent Partner in the Advancement of Measurement and Assessment Practices (A Student-Centered Assessment

Model)." Paper presented at the Winter Institute on Community College Effectiveness and Student Success, Jacksonville, Fla., Jan. 27, 1992. 10 pp. (ED 342 446)

Michigan's Macomb Community College's institutional assessment model involves using technology to collect and disseminate data on student learning in order to facilitate continuous improvement and adaptation. The first element of this five-part model is the mandatory testing, orientation, and placement of incoming students. Using placement test scores, course grades, and placement recommendations, computer programs analyze the comparative success and retention rates of students who do and do not follow placement recommendations. The second part of the model relates student learning outcomes to course objectives. A computerized early warning system uses faculty input to identify students at risk of failure during the first weeks of each semester and passes on suggestions for improved attendance or additional counseling. The third element is long-term monitoring. Each student's program is regularly analyzed and updated by the computer, not only in terms of progress toward a degree, but also with regard to fulfilling transfer requirements. The fourth element is exit competency assessment, using pre- and posttests to measure student gains after two years. The fifth element of data collection focuses on transfer and employment.

Calhoun, H. D. "The Nichols Institutional Effectiveness Model and Its Adaptation at Jefferson State Community College." Paper presented at the 73rd Annual National Convention of the American Association of Community Colleges, Portland, Oreg., Apr. 28–May 1, 1993. 7 pp. (ED 357 785)

The Nichols Institutional Effectiveness (NIE) paradigm is a practical guide to implementing effectiveness efforts that fits most accreditation requirements, focuses on assessment results instead of processes, makes the institutional mission the basis for assessment, and raises the level of analysis to the institutional level. In addition, the NIE model includes four critical elements: the establishment of an expanded statement of institutional purpose, including goals and mission; an identification of intended results for all functions of the institution; an assessment of the extent to which these results are achieved; and adjustments made on the basis of assessment findings. After the initial implementation process, an annual cycle must be established so that the activities are integrated into the normal efforts of the institution.

Seppanen, L. *The Washington Community College Institutional Outcomes Assessment Plans: An Overview and Summary. Operations Research no. 91–2.* Olympia: Washington State Board for Community College Education, 1991. 54 pp. (ED 345 789)

In 1990, pursuant to the Washington community college system's request, the Washington state legislature appropriated additional funding to pursue assessment at the local college level as a way to address issues of institutional improvement. Each college submitted preliminary plans to the State Board for Community College Education, which gave the colleges feedback about their plans, providing suggestions for revisions and improvements where appropriate. Colleges were asked to follow a particular format in their final plans, addressing a series of questions designed to elicit a full and accurate picture of their 1990–1991 assessment process. This report presents a compilation and summary of the assessment plans of all twenty-seven colleges in the system.

Assessment as a Planning Tool

Institutional assessment has been used as an aid to long-range planning.

Cannon, D. T., and others. "Institutional Improvement: Making Assessment Work for You." Paper presented at the Third Annual Effectiveness and Student Success Conference, Greensboro, N.C., June 23–25, 1991. 20 pp. (ED 332 759)
   Drawing from the experiences of South Carolina's Midlands Technical College (MTC), this paper offers guidelines for operationalizing institutional effectiveness and presents selected findings from MTC's efforts to assess institutional outcomes. After summarizing MTC's method for operationalizing institutional effectiveness, the paper describes MTC's academic program assessment system and efforts to build student success and college effectiveness through retention tracking. Findings from these studies and the methods used to communicate results of effectiveness measures within the college are also reviewed.

Grunder, P. *Measuring Institutional Effectiveness Through the Strategic Planning Process.* Gainesville, Fla.: Santa Fe Community College, 1991. 27 pp. (ED 336 134)
   Designed to assist faculty, staff, and administrators in understanding the strategic planning process at Florida's Santa Fe Community College and to help them develop guidelines to measure the effectiveness of their unit, department, or administrative area, this report outlines the key missions of the community college, presents sample criteria and measures specific to the strategic planning process, and includes an institutional self-assessment instrument.

Hudgins, J. *Institutional Effectiveness: A Strategy for Institutional Renewal.* Columbia, S.C.: Midlands Technical College, 1991. 13 pp. (ED 335 087)
   Efforts to assess institutional effectiveness not only enable community colleges to meet accreditation mandates, but can also serve as a catalyst for institutional renewal. Institutional effectiveness has become an important topic for the 1990s as a result of past neglect of accountability, new legislative mandates

for education, changes in accreditation criteria from process-oriented to outcomes-oriented, and a renewed interest on the part of colleges in improving the quality of instruction. To assess institutional effectiveness, a college must define the mission of the college; articulate the major results that are expected from the achievement of the mission; and determine the specific evidence that will be acceptable to determine whether those results have been achieved. At a minimum, institutional assessment processes require that institutions articulate their mission, establish a planning mechanism, develop an evaluation system, identify critical areas of success, establish priority standards on which the college can judge its effectiveness, determine mechanisms for documenting whether the established standards have been met, and use the results of assessment for decision making.

Leas, D., and Lillibridge, F. "Institutional Assessment, Planning, and Institutional Change: An Integrated Institutional Assessment and Strategic Planning Process for Community Colleges." Paper presented at the 14th National Institute for Staff and Organizational Development International Conference on Teaching Excellence, Austin, Tex., May 24–27, 1992. 24 pp. (ED 360 000)

In 1992, Alamogordo Branch Community College (ABCC), a branch campus of New Mexico State University, developed and implemented the Institutional Assessment and Strategic Planning (IASP) process, an integrated process designed to assess both student academic achievement and institutional effectiveness. Each year, the IASP process begins when individual faculty members evaluate their assessment activities for all courses and complete reports about their assessment efforts. Next, instructors in all academic disciplines discuss their assessment activities at discipline-specific focus group meetings. Other activities include focus groups among each of the four academic divisions, focus retreats for faculty and for student services personnel, focus group meetings in each student service program, and institutional and instructional support focus groups and retreats. At focus group meetings, participants complete forms listing strengths and concerns in their areas and develop action plans. The IASP committee uses these forms and actions to develop a set of institutional issues. The issues are ranked, actions are developed to address each issue, and an overall institutional plan is developed and presented to the college community. The IASP process is successful at ABCC because it provides an opportunity for everyone on campus to be heard.

Marrow, A. J., and Reed, R. "College Renewal through the Self-Study Process." Paper presented at the League for Innovation in the Community College "Leadership 2000" conference, Chicago, July 8, 1991. 35 pp. (ED 337 210)

In May 1989, as part of a college renewal and self-study process, Hazard Community College conducted a two-day retreat involving all segments of the college community. At the end of the second day, each of the eleven focus groups presented a consensus of its views to the entire college community. The lists of values generated by the groups, focusing on topics such as programs, finance, and interpersonal relations, were consolidated into a summary of values (SOV), which was distributed to every retreat participant. Following the retreat, an institutional purpose committee was established to rewrite the college's statement of purpose and the SOV in order to translate them into seventeen institutional goals. Through a series of public forums, these goals were presented to faculty, support staff, administration, students, and the community. Based on these forums, a revised mission statement was prepared and submitted to the entire college community and to the college's advisory board for approval.

Myers, C. J., and Silvers, P. J. "Evaluating the College Mission Through Assessing Institutional Outcomes." Paper presented at the 33rd annual forum of the Association for Institutional Research, Chicago, May 16–19, 1993. 13 pp. (ED 357 773)

To develop a new mission statement for Pima Community College (PCC) in Tucson, Arizona, a "charette" process was used in which detailed community input was solicited and incorporated as part of the mission statement development. After the initial charette, the same group convened several months later to develop a set of outcomes, or indicators of success, directly linked to each of the twelve major areas of the college mission. After this second charette, PCC's chancellor appointed an editorial committee of six representative charette participants. In the ensuing months, an institutional effectiveness committee (IEC), made up of administrators, faculty, and staff, prescribed one or more specific measures to assess each indicator of success. For each measure, the IEC listed a success criterion, data source, and timeline for collecting data. The resulting specifications table served as the basis for the collection, analysis, and reporting of assessment information. In May 1992, PCC's first annual report to the community was conducted, in which assessment results were presented to the original charette groups.

Student Outcome Studies

Student outcomes are an important criterion for consideration during the assessment process.

Kreider, P. E., and others. *Institutional Effectiveness and Student Success.* Gresham, Oreg.: Mount Hood Community College, 1993. 20 pp. (ED 356 843)

Mount Hood Community College (MHCC) has instituted an ongoing systematic review of instructional program improvement and implemented institutional strategic planning directly linked to budget development. To help assess student success, MHCC has collected student intent data on entry and on a term-by-term basis since 1983, focussing on educational and career goals and intended duration at MHCC. Also, the college instituted a mandatory assessment and placement program in 1984 to enhance the prospects of student success. At the core of MHCC's institutional effectiveness assessment is the program review process, conducted on an annual basis and using such quantitative and qualitative indicators as student demand, job placement, transfer success, the local employment outlook, and staff development. Results of program review activities are incorporated into the annual strategic planning process, a participatory effort that engenders community dialogue and provides the basis for the budget development process.

Lee, B. S. *Measures of Progress: Student Follow-Up, Spring 1991 (with Selected Trends, 1984–1991)*. Sacramento, Calif.: Office of Planning and Research, Los Rios Community College District, 1992. 24 pp. (ED 344 648)

The Los Rios Community College (LRCC) District conducted student follow-up surveys annually from 1984 through 1987 and biennially since then. These surveys are designed to determine the educational goals of the students, current employment or educational status, and whether LRCC's offerings had met their individual needs. The spring 1991 survey was mailed to 5,744 former students, and responses were returned by 2,541. Respondents included 1,087 students whose goal was primarily to earn university transfer credit, 649 occupational preparation students, 324 occupational retraining students, and 481 personal interest students. Study findings included the following: (1) almost 69 percent of the students who enrolled to earn transfer credit had transferred to a university by the time of the survey, and almost 68 percent of this group were employed; (2) among the respondents who had enrolled to prepare for a new job, more than 84 percent were employed, and 76 percent of the employed respondents who provided employment data were working in jobs related to their community college training; (3) of the group who had enrolled to improve existing job skills, more than 53 percent had earned an associate degree or certificate; and (4) among the respondents who had enrolled for personal interest reasons, more than 15 percent had re-enrolled in a community college, 16 percent had transferred to a four-year college, and 66 percent had earned an associate degree or certificate.

Lutz, D. A. *Student Outcomes Assessment: Are We as Good as We Think?* Iowa City, Iowa: American College Testing Program, 1992. 96 pp. (ED 354 930)

In order to evaluate the validity of outcomes assessment at two-year colleges, the American College Testing (ACT) Program developed Project Cooperation. Institutions participating in the project administered tests and surveys to measure changes in students' cognitive abilities over time and record student feedback, and reported the data along with curricula and student transcript information to ACT. To measure cognitive outcomes, seventy-eight colleges applied the Collegiate Assessment of Academic Proficiency test to first-year students in 1989 and 1990 and again to the same students in 1992. To gather student feedback, seventy-two participating institutions administered the College Outcomes Survey (COS) in spring 1992. The COS includes sections on student background, college outcomes or goals, student evaluation of the importance of each outcome or goal, student progress in all areas, and student satisfaction. Results of the assessment of student feedback included the following: (1) acquiring knowledge and skills in an area of specialization ranked as the highest goal and as the area of most progress; (2) students responded positively towards colleges' general education programs; and (3) the areas of highest satisfaction were class size and response to older and nontraditional students.

Spartanburg Technical College. *Guidelines for Implementation of Outcomes Assessment.* Spartanburg, S.C.: Spartanburg Technical College, 1991. 68 pp. (ED 331 385)

This manual addresses the specific needs of Spartanburg Technical College in evaluating student outcomes of program competencies. The guidelines provide a step-by-step method for faculty to evaluate the objectives by which they teach and the assessment methods they use to measure students' achievement of those objectives. A four-part evaluation process is outlined: (1) analyze course competencies and objectives to determine their domain (cognitive, psychomotor, affective) and level (knowledge, application, problem solving); (2) analyze the assessment methods used in order to test those competencies and objectives in the same domains and levels of the assessment instrument; (3) compare the levels of the domains found in the course objectives with those found in the assessment instruments; (4) change assessment instruments that do not match the levels of the course objectives, or create new assessment instruments.

Yao, M. *Assessing Student Outcomes via Follow-Up Survey: Training Effectiveness of Vancouver Community College.* Vancouver, B.C.: Vancouver Community College, 1993. 19 pp. (ED 357 815)

For the 1990–1991 survey, 3,685 graduates were surveyed nine months after program completion and 1,007 discontinuants were surveyed one month after a withdrawal record appeared in the students' record. The survey sought information on former students' characteristics, training-related work experience before coming to Vancouver Community College (VCC), financial sources for education, main objective for enrolling in an occupational program at VCC, the extent to which students met their objectives, employment status and rate, reasons for unemployment, reasons for not being employed in training-related fields, quality of preparation for employment or transfer, usefulness of VCC training, quality of equipment, transfer problems, educational plans, and overall rating of VCC training. Study findings, based on responses from 32 percent of the program completers and 25 percent of the discontinuants, included the following: (1) 55 percent of the graduates attended VCC to learn the skills needed for a job and 17 percent attended to improve existing job skills; (2) 91 percent felt that they met their objectives by attending VCC; (3) 55 percent of the graduates were employed full-time nine months after graduation and another 26 percent were employed part-time; (4) 84 percent of the graduates sought employment related to their training; (5) of the unemployed graduates, 21 percent reported that they needed more education or training to obtain jobs; and (6) almost all respondents rated their training as either definitely worthwhile (67 percent) or worthwhile to some extent (30 percent).

ELIZABETH FOOTE is user services coordinator at the ERIC Clearinghouse for Community Colleges, University of California, Los Angeles.

INDEX

ORDERING INFORMATION

NEW DIRECTIONS FOR COMMUNITY COLLEGES is a series of paperback books that provides expert assistance to help community colleges meet the challenges of their distinctive and expanding educational mission. Books in the series are published quarterly in Spring, Summer, Fall, and Winter and are available for purchase by subscription and individually.

SUBSCRIPTIONS for 1994 cost $49.00 for individuals (a savings of more than 25 percent over single-copy prices) and $72.00 for institutions, agencies, and libraries. Please do not send institutional checks for personal subscriptions. Standing orders are accepted.

SINGLE COPIES cost $16.95 when payment accompanies order. (California, New Jersey, New York, and Washington, D.C., residents please include appropriate sales tax.) Billed orders will be charged postage and handling.

DISCOUNTS FOR QUANTITY ORDERS are available. Please write to the address below for information.

ALL ORDERS must include either the name of an individual or an official purchase order number. Please submit your order as follows:
    Subscriptions: specify series and year subscription is to begin
    Single copies: include individual title code (such as CC82)

MAIL ALL ORDERS TO:
    Jossey-Bass Publishers
    350 Sansome Street
    San Francisco, California 94104-1342

FOR SUBSCRIPTION SALES OUTSIDE OF THE UNITED STATES, contact any international subscription agency or Jossey-Bass directly.